THE SPIRIT
OF MUSIC

A MISSIONARY TOOL

THE SPIRIT
OF MUSIC

A MISSIONARY TOOL

Lela Guymon Christensen

Alto No. 62

Mormon Tabernacle Choir

ISBN: 1-55517-093-5
Library of Congress
Catalog Card Number: 93-071171

Published and distributed by:

CFI
Cedar Fort, Incorporated
925 North Main, Springville, UT 84663 801-489-4084

This book is not an official publication of The Church of Jesus
Christ of Latter-day Saints. All opinions expressed herein are the
author's and are not necessarily those of the publisher or of The
Church of Jesus Christ of Latter-day Saints.

Cover Design by Lyle Mortimer
Typeset by Brian Carter
Lithographed in the United States of America

In Appreciation

My love and appreciation

go to my husband Kurt,

our children, Linda, Alan, Ronald, Dean,

Susan, Keith, Kay, and Robert (Bob);

also to their spouses and our grandchildren

for all their encouragement and support

during my years as a member of

the Mormon Tabernacle Choir.

Special thanks and love to my parents,

Lafayette and Winnie Guymon,

for my musical training.

I am grateful to my bishop, Joseph Walker,

and Iris Syndergaard, editor,

for their suggestions and encouragement.

All royalties go to a missionary fund.

Table of Contents

Prelude

The Mormon Tabernacle Choir is the Lord's emissary, opening doors for the LDS missionaries throughout the world.

Members of the Mormon Tabernacle Choir share many spiritual missionary experiences together. Events happen naturally, but in retrospect choir members see the Lord's hand in events which have taken place. Each choir member's experience is unique, but still one we all share together.

While in Japan, my husband Kurt wrote in his personal journal, "This is a great and marvelous missionary opportunity for our church and most powerful. Motivating my writing today is the response of the people at the choir performances. It is such a deeply moving experience that I wonder how to preserve it in writing, for nothing can be said to record the real spirit of the occasion. It is like describing a sunset to one who was not there to drink in the view."

Music—A Universal Language

Letters arrive from all over the world at the Mormon Tabernacle Choir office, located in Salt Lake City, Utah, telling of the choir's influence on people's lives and of their conversion to the church. Letters will say, "I want to join the Mormon Tabernacle Choir Church," or "I'm a member of the Mormon Tabernacle Choir Church and listen faithfully every Sunday to the broadcast of 'Music and the Spoken Word.'" These "golden letters" are given to the Church's Missionary Department.

"Just as John the Baptist was the forerunner of Jesus Christ for His ministry, Joseph Smith was forerunner of the gospel in the latter days, so now is the Mormon Tabernacle Choir a forerunner of the Latter-day Saint (LDS) missionaries to take the gospel message worldwide." This statement was made by our choir president, Wendell Smoot, as he set me apart for my missionary calling with the Mormon Tabernacle Choir.

The Tabernacle Choir is sent to areas throughout the world, opening doors for our missionaries, lifting and strengthening, helping break down barriers of resistance to the church. Publicity preceding the arrival of the choir in a country, for our concerts and our television appearances, will reach millions of people before a tour is over.

Performances also draw picketers and demonstrators against the choir and the Church. Picketers were shipped from America to Scandinavian countries to pass out anti-Mormon literature at the end of our concerts there. Prominent people and organizations have tried to block performances of the choir, but these are as a small thorn prick, hardly felt. They try to stop the work of the Lord, but in truth, help further the work of the missionaries by drawing attention to the choir, and people want to know more.

At choir concerts, programs passed out to the audience not only tell about choir activities, but also list questions and answers about the choir and the church it represents. Referral cards found in the brochure can be filled out by investigators who are interested in learning more. Many cards are filled out, signed by non-members, and dropped in boxes provided by our missionaries in the foyer as the audience leaves the concert hall. LDS missionaries act as ushers—ready and willing to answer any questions about the choir and the Church of Jesus Christ of Latter-day Saints. On the Tabernacle Choir's first tour to Japan, so many boxes were filled with referral cards that it took missionaries several months to contact and teach all of the people who wanted to hear more about the gospel.

Radio and television stations around the world broadcast the general conference of the Church. The Mormon Tabernacle Choir is an integral part of each conference. Singing for conference is one of the main functions of the choir. It helps open the hearts of the people so the gospel can be taught.

President David O. McKay said, "Music is a universal language." Music will reach through a language barrier just as a smile or frown can be understood without words.

Have you ever attended a concert where a guest soloist is from another country? He cannot speak your language, but you feel what he is feeling, sitting spellbound, enthralled with music pouring forth form the artist to the listener, reaching the heart with its power to uplift and motivate lives.

A letter, read to the choir before a Sunday morning broadcast from Temple Square in Salt Lake City, told of a man living in the eastern states who had become very depressed. His wife was suing for a divorce. His children had lost respect for him as they watched their father drink, sinking lower and lower, until he lost his job. This man's family left him—he was living alone.

One Sunday morning, gun in hand, he turned on the television to cover the sound of a shot. But music floated through the air as the Mormon Tabernacle Choir sang its weekly broadcast. Pausing, he listened to "Music and the Spoken Word." As the broadcast ended, instead of lifting the gun to his head, he looked up the "Church of Jesus Christ of Latter-day Saints" in the telephone book, lifted up the telephone receiver, and called the LDS mission home for help. This man is now a faithful member of the church. Music reached his heart and saved a life.

A letter delivered to the choir office from Africa read on the envelope, "The Choir, United States of America." No other address was on the letter, but it still arrived at the correct destination—its contents shared with the choir.

Recently, two letters came to the choir office. At Sunday morning rehearsal we were told about the conversion of two different families, one in Puerto Rico and one in the West Indies. Their stories were similar.

Two missionaries in Puerto Rico had tracted all day with little success when they were impressed to go to a house and knock. A lady answering the door, hearing they represented the Church of Jesus Christ of Latter-day Saints, commonly known as the "Mormon" church, invited the young men in. She told the missionaries she had Christmas recordings of the choir. In fact, she had numerous records of the Tabernacle Choir in her home. Talking of the choir and its music opened the door. She and her family listened to the missionary lessons, and afterwards asked for baptism.

In the West Indies, two missionaries were at the end of a discouraging day of tracting when they were impressed to stop at a house and knock. The missionaries introduced themselves to the lady answering the door and told her about the church they represented. She asked if it was the same church the Mormon Tabernacle Choir belonged to. The missionaries said yes. She immediately invited them in and told them she owned several choir records. She had listened to the music many times, and as she listened, she had felt that the church the choir belonged to was the true church. She asked the missionaries to baptize her. The missionaries told her she could be baptized, but first they would teach her the missionary lessons so she would know the true principles of the gospel. She and her family listened and learned. When the lessons were completed, they were all baptized and are now faithful members of the Church.

An LDS missionary who had served a mission to the Philippines wrote of the persecution he and his companion had experienced in one town. A minister of another faith had become so bitter against the Mormon missionaries that he started a very effective campaign to smear the reputation of those teaching the Mormon doctrines. Anti-Mormon articles appeared in newspapers and loudspeaker trucks boomed voices speaking against the Church outside LDS meetinghouses. An attempt was made by car to run down missionaries walking on a road. This minister had published anti-Mormon literature. He then attempted to acquire radio air time in his campaign against the church.

In the meantime, our missionaries had left choir music and broadcast tapes with the owner of the local radio station. The manager reluctantly agreed to hear the choir broadcast tapes and decide whether they would be useable on the air. The next day our missionaries went back to the station, fully expecting the owner to hand the tapes back and show them the door. To their surprise, they were warmly greeted and invited into his office where he explained that he had been warned about Mormons by the minister. The minister had made many unkind and false statements about the Mormons and their missionaries. The station owner said he had been very reluctant to even take the tapes to listen to. But after listening to "Music and the Spoken Word," he knew the words of the minister were not true and felt in his heart that the choir's message represented God's Church on earth. He apologized.

As our missionaries left, they were asked for more choir broadcast tapes. The station owner began a program heard nightly over the air called the "Mormon Hour." Antagonism in the town melted away. Many doors were opened to the missionaries so they could preach the gospel.

Through the broadcasts the choir's influence expanded to other areas of the world. Nicaragua presented a gift to the choir in the form of a commemerative stamp on which the choir is pictured. For a country to honor the choir in such a way is truly remarkable, especially considering we have only been heard by broadcast. The stamp was later duplicated, incased in plastic and made into paperweights for each choir member.

Helen Keller visited a choir rehearsal while she was in Salt Lake City. How would she be able to listen to music, being not only blind but unable to hear?

Having been escorted down underneath the choir loft to the rooms below, she placed her hands on the wood walls underneath the choir and tabernacle organ. She could feel the vibrations of the music in the wood. With tears in her eyes, she said it was one of the most marvelous experiences of her life as she felt the music through her fingers. The music reached her very soul.

Recently, a mother and her young daughter visited a Sunday morning broadcast. A few weeks later, a letter arrived from the mother telling the choir of their experience. The mother said her daughter had never seen a river or a mountain stream—she was blind.

As part of our broadcast, the choir had sung "Waters Ripple and Flow." During the song, the mother looked over at her daughter and saw tears streaming down her face. After the broadcast, she put an arm around her daughter asking the reason for her tears. Her daughter was full of happiness, saying, "For the first time I can see water ripple and flow."

Choir members seldom know at the time we are singing the effect our music has had on our audience or the doors we are opening for the missionaries. Later, we are sometimes told individually or collectively about the joy our music brought into the lives of those listening. It is a very humbling experience to realize the influence and impact our music has had on the lives of people in their conversion to the gospel.

Washington, D.C.—
Music for the Nation

President-elect Lyndon Johnson invited the Mormon Tabernacle Choir to sing at his inauguration January 10, 1965. What a thrill to sing my first concert with the choir away from home and at a presidential inauguration.

Fog grounded our planes at the Salt Lake Airport. Orders were given by airport officials to seed the fog. It worked, but just long enough to allow one plane to take off with our technical crew and choir leadership aboard. If this plane had not arrived in Washington ahead of time, the Mormon Tabernacle Choir could not have sung at the inauguration. Sound systems had to be wired by our technical crew and final arrangements co-ordinated, so the choir's performance could be seen, heard, and televised.

Unable to fly out from the Salt Lake Airport, the main body of the choir was bused to McCarren Airport in Las Vegas, only to find flight crews grounded. They had just flown in from another assignment and flight regulations required them to rest. We lost two more hours before they could fly again.

Finally, arriving in Washington, D.C., a police escort stopped all traffic for nine choir buses weaving back and forth from one side of the road to the other, dodging traffic, frantically racing to the Chevy Chase Ward chapel. Quickly changing into concert dress, we hopped back on buses and drove like mad, arriving at the nation's Capitol. We had just one-half hour to find our places, make our sound check, and be ready to sing.

Our risers were to be the steps of the Capitol. Being bitter cold weather, we wore thermals under our concert clothes. Heat lamps warmed Alexander Schreiner's fingers and the piano keyboard.

The press had been moved from their good vantage point on the Capitol steps to directly in front of the choir on the bottom level. Disgruntled and unhappy, their body actions and faces portrayed dislike at being moved further away from where the inaugural activities were taking place. I was on the front row, only one foot away from where reporters were sitting facing us, my foot almost touching the newspaper reporter's foot in front of me. Not a smile could be seen on any of their faces. I smiled at them, but their response was a cold blank expression.

Beginning the ceremonies, the choir sang "This is My Country," and interspersed through the program, we sang other patriotic songs. After the inauguration of President Johnson, we sang "Battle Hymn of the Republic." Instantaneous, thunderous clapping and shouting burst forth from the crowd, with front row journalists being first to jump up shouting, "Bravo, bravo, bravo."

Starting to walk back to our buses, several reporters and other spectators stopped my friends and I. They smiled, and with great enthusiasm, complimented the choir for its stirring performance.

Flying home by jet plane at 600 miles an hour, choir members were very tired after 48 hours without sleep. We were glad to rest, close our eyes, and wait for food to be prepared. But this was not to be. Our flight crew decided to have announced over the intercom of the plane "We are not serving food until you sing for your supper," and opened the cooking ovens to let the aroma of food filter throughout the plane. "Smells good— doesn't it," laughed the stewardess. "There is only one way we will serve your food—you must first sing for your supper." Groaning, very tired, but also very hungry, such a delicious aroma of food filtering through the plane, we sang three songs from the inaugural program, finishing with, "Come, Come Ye Saints."

While we were singing "Come, Come Ye Saints," I thought of my pioneer grandparents who had crossed the plains, driven from their homes in Nauvoo, and of the long trek across America to the valley of the Great Salt Lake. Kurt's great uncle, C.C.A. Christensen, depicted this mass exodus in paintings now displayed in museums and published in history books. The early saints were persecuted for their religious beliefs, and now the choir was flying home over this same route, having just been honored by our nation.

The flight crew finally served dinner, and after, we fell into blessed sleep.

Approaching Denver, our pilot announced over the intercom that Salt Lake Airport was still covered over with fog—we would land in Denver to take a train the rest of the way home. A few minutes passed when we heard again on the loudspeaker, "It's only an hour to Salt Lake. Why don't we fly over and take a look to see if there is a chance of landing." As we approached the Salt Lake Airport, an opening was seen in the fog, runway lights glittered below and our planes landed.

Kurt said that as he and the children left our home in Bountiful, Utah, fog was very thick and stayed that way until just before they reached the airport. Then he saw the fog thin out, leaving an opening in the sky above the runway as our planes landed. We were the first planes to land in several days. After the choir planes touched down, the fog closed in. No more planes were able to land or take off.

Our family arrived home just in time to turn on the television and see the 10 p.m. news showing the Mormon Tabernacle Choir singing at the inauguration ceremonies, myself on the front row.

The choir members all knew the Lord had given us a special blessing making it possible to sing at inaugural time in Washington, D.C.

President Johnson phoned President David O. McKay to express his appreciation for the beautiful patriotic music sung by the choir. Later, President Johnson gave the flag which had flown over the House of Representatives during the inauguration to President McKay as a thank you for the choir's participation in the ceremonies.

The choir was invited back to Washington D.C. for the 47th annual National Christmas Tree Lighting Ceremony at the White House in December 1970. This time it was not fog, but snow causing problems. It would be one wet trip.

Choir members boarded planes for takeoff from the Salt Lake Airport. Our plane taxied to the end of the runway, the final instrument check being made by our flight crew. The prayer was being said over the intercom, asking the Lord for protection, that we would have a safe flight and also sing well at our upcoming performance.

Within a minute or two after the prayer was completed, the pilot found mechanical difficulty with our plane. If it had taken off the results could have been disastrous—our plane might have crashed. We taxied off the runway back to the Salt Lake air terminal.

After a short delay, airline officials provided a smaller plane. It was announced that if any choir members would rather stay home, they could. Enough choir members raised their hands to solve the problem of seating capacity. The balance of the choir boarded the smaller plane and took off for Washington D.C.

Because of the delay, our plane load of choir members was too far behind schedule to go change into concert dress and be at the Washington Monument in time to perform. Dress bags were at the back of the plane. It was decided the only way we could change into concert dress was on the plane—ladies to the front and men to the tail of the plane with their backs to each other. It worked!

Choir leadership knew ahead of time there was a good possibility of storm, so plastic cleaning bags were provided to go under our concert dress to help keep us dry. We cut holes in the top of the plastic bag for our head and arms and slipped them on under our concert clothes just in time for the "fasten your seat belt" sign to come on, alerting us it was time to land. We descended in a blinding snow storm—a very bumpy ride. It continued snowing all through the outdoor Christmas tree lighting ceremony. Our music folders and outer clothing were soaked. After singing, the choir was invited into the warm White House, given a conducted tour, then bused back to the airport.

At home the next day, I ironed water-damaged, crinkled music with a steam iron before going to rehearsal in the Tabernacle. The music was a little worse for the wear, but the choir arrived home safely and our prayers answered.

For President Nixon's inauguration, I remained home in Salt Lake watching the choir being televised from Washington, D.C. We were expecting our eighth child. It was a different experience watching the choir and not performing.

In September 1974 the choir performed a concert under the direction of our new choir conductor, Jay Welch, at the Kennedy Center in Washington, D.C. After the concert, President Gerald Ford and his wife came on stage to greet the choir. It was a treat to meet them, but even more special was a concert in the Kennedy Center on July 3, 1976.

The choir had a two-fold purpose in Washington; first, to sing at the dedication ceremonies of the Washington, D.C. Temple Visitors Center where President Spencer W. Kimball gave the dedicatory prayer and second, to sing in the Kennedy Center, taking part in the nation's Bicentennial Celebration.

On July 3rd, the "Honor America" program was presented at the Kennedy Center. Opening prayer was given by Billy Graham. Many of our nation's top performers were on the program. Art Linkletter was master of ceremonies. He kept patting my shoulder as he came off the stage where I sat on an end seat. Bob Hope, Telly Savalas, O.J. Simpson, Annette Funicello, George Kennedy, the U.S. Army Herald Trumpets, the Joint Armed Forces Color Guard and the Mormon Tabernacle Choir all took part on the program. This was quite an impressive array of top talent.

President Gerald Ford gave the Bicentennial message, but the most outstanding event to me, and one I will always remember, occurred when President Ford, President Spencer W. Kimball, and their wives walked down the stairway together into the Presidential Box, sitting side by side—the President of the Church and the president of our nation watching our program together.

The next day was the 4th of July. The choir sang as part of the nationally televised "Happy Birthday, America" program at the Washington monument.

The audience extended as far as you could see. Temporary fences were erected between the choir and the audience. Mounted police patrolled the area. It was quite a sight. After the program that night, choir members quickly boarded buses back to the airport as firework displays began to burst in the sky.

January 17, 1981, the Mormon Tabernacle Choir was invited again to Washington, D.C. to sing for the inauguration of President Ronald Reagan. Hotels are full at inauguration time and the nation's capital was "jam packed." The choir generally will stay at a hotel when we travel, but this time gracious people in the surrounding area opened their homes for choir members to stay the four days we would be in Washington. My host family, the Ed Duvall's, drove us to their home in Virginia, a short distance from the capital where my partner and I enjoyed their hospitality. They are a special family.

The question is often asked, "Who pays for choir trips?" The answer is, neither the government nor the Church pay our expenses. The choir is self-sustaining. We pay our own way from the proceeds of concert tickets, record royalties, and private contributions.

The next morning, zero weather made it very cold in Washington and it felt even colder as the choir stood on the steps of the Lincoln Memorial ready to practice and sing with the United States Army Band at the opening inauguration ceremonies.

In front of the steps, on a temporary stage, chairs were set up for the band and President-elect Reagan and his party. Small cans filled with fire were strategically placed among the band members to prevent their instrument valves and slides from freezing and sticking. During a rehearsal break, choir members would move down to the band to warm themselves and visit by the small fires, then move back to the bitter cold steps.

After a short break, the opening inaugural program began. The United States Army Band played as Efrem Zimbalist, Jr., master of ceremonies, announced the arrival of Vice-President-elect George Bush and his wife. The choir parted down the middle making an aisle from the top, by the Lincoln statue. Mr.

Bush and his wife began descending the steps to take their place on stage. A minute later was heard, "Ladies and gentlemen, President-elect of the United States of America, Ronald Reagan and his wife, Nancy Reagan." We looked up and watched as Mr. and Mrs. Reagan descended the stairs through the center of the choir, crossed in front, smiled at the choir and gave us a friendly wave, then took their places by Vice President Bush and his wife.

At a signal and by request, the choir began singing softly "God of Our Fathers," as the opening prayer was given by a bishop from the Greek Orthodox Church. After the prayer, church bells could be heard from all over Washington. We then sang our National Anthem, "The Star-Spangled Banner," accompanied by the band. As we sang the words, "bombs bursting in air," cannons shot off, fireworks burst above and around us, then flags of all the states were carried and placed on stage by men in colonial costumes. After being introduced, Mr. Reagan and Mr. Bush spoke to the people of the nation. Several patriotic songs were sung by the choir with band accompaniment. At strategic points in the program, cannon blasts could be heard and fireworks seen bursting above us.

At the conclusion of the opening ceremonies, Mr. Reagan and his party walked back across the stage and stopped directly in front of me. He smiled, shook hands with three of us and said,"Thank you for such a stirring performance." He expressed his appreciation for the choir being in Washington as part of his inauguration ceremonies, smiled again and waved at all the choir as he and his party proceeded up the steps through the center of the choir and disappeared over the top by the statue of Lincoln as fireworks burst in all directions, church bells rang, and cannons shot off a salute to the president-elect. It was a once-in-a-lifetime experience.

Sunday morning dawned bright and clear the next day. The choir was invited to broadcast "Music and the Spoken Word" from the sanctuary of the Washington Hebrew Congregation Church. Invited guests at the broadcast were VIPs of Washington. I was told that only one person was unable to attend.

The acoustics of the synagogue were similar to the acoustics in the Tabernacle back home in Salt Lake City. This gave our guests the added treat of hearing the choir sing with the same sound that visitors hear in the Tabernacle. It is a different sound than that of a record album or a concert not in the Tabernacle. In the Tabernacle the musical sound is more complete and full.

At the synagogue, our guests sat in the balcony and the back seats on the main floor. The choir occupied the front congregational seats with an aisle dividing the two sections of seats in the middle. For broadcast purposes, the choir sang with our backs to the audience. After the broadcast, we turned to our audience and sang a mini-concert.

As the last note was sung, I could see many handkerchiefs wiping many eyes. The applause was loud and spontaneous, a call for more.

Standing by the edge of the middle aisle, I gathered up my music to leave when Chief Justice Warren Burger of the Supreme Court hurried toward me down the aisle on his way to see Jerold Ottley. But as he came down the aisle, he paused, grabbed me by both shoulders, and with tears streaming down his face said, "The music was beautiful, just great, just great. The people of Washington really heard you sing. The choir sounded just like they do in the Tabernacle." He gave me a big bear hug, wiped his eyes, and continued to the front where Jerold Ottley was standing and hugged Jerry, expressing his feelings and gratitude for the choir's performance.

As this experience was happening to me, the same thing was happening to one of my friends in the choir. A man with tears in his eyes expressed his joy to my friend. He had been very moved by the choir's music, had become emotional, and had difficulty speaking. After he had left, a gentleman who had stood next to this man asked my friend if she knew the person she had been speaking to. Of course she said, "no." The gentleman then informed her, "The man you have just talked to was the ambassador for the Soviet Union." It was the first time he had seen the ambassador so emotionally moved since he had been in Washington.

On inauguration day, the choir boarded a 14-foot-wide and 110-foot-long float. It had a swivel in the middle so corners on the parade route could be turned. Sitting in double mixed-quartet formation, eight across on each row, the choir was spread out for almost a block. Since the weather was very cold, our choir president, Oakley Evans, decided we should wear our coats, even though we had concert clothes on underneath.

Utah's governor, Scott Matheson, and his wife, Norma, after looking for us for two hours, finally located our float and told us how proud the state of Utah was to have the Mormon Tabernacle Choir represent the western states of America. Only four floats were in the parade, each representing a portion of the United States.

Just before time arrived for the float to move down the parade route, it felt warm and we were told to take off our coats. We could be seen in concert dress after all. Loudspeakers mounted under the float made it possible for the choir to sing with its own recordings, giving emphasis to the music of "America the Beautiful," "You're a Grand Old Flag," "God Bless America," "Marching Along Together, and "Battle Hymn of the Republic." Moving down the street, crowds waved and cheered on all sides. It was planned that we sing at intervals along the parade route, but as we stopped singing, people sitting in the stands built along the streets, realized we were not going to sing in front of them, shouted, "Sing, sing." Jerry smiled and said to the choir, "OK, we will sing all the way." People cheered, clapped, and waved small flags, our music enthusiastically received.

Looking behind our float, which was last in the parade, I could see people for two blocks following our float to hear the choir sing. It looked like a full stadium of people on a ball field. At one side of our float we had Sonja Johnson and her followers picketing. (In fact they were everywhere we went, including our visit to the Washington, D.C. Temple.) But before we were done, they were cheering with the rest of the crowd. The crowd became so great behind us that the military marching unit in front of our float broke ranks every so often and formed a line across the street keeping back the crowds so we could move on, then returned to their formation in front of us and continued marching.

The choir began singing "Battle Hymn of the Republic" as we approached the presidential reviewing stand. Our float stopped and we continued singing. My position—twelve rows from the front on the side close to where President Reagan and his wife stood—gave me a close-up view of the president stretching over to reach his wife's hand. He missed, then leaned, and finally grasped her hand. They looked at each other, tears on their faces, then turned back, and continued to listen with moist eyes as we sang. In contrast, Vice-President Bush and his wife beamed from ear to ear, singing along with us. Behind them stood President Reagan's brother mopping tears from his eyes with a big handkerchief. At the conclusion of "Battle Hymn," we waved goodbye and began singing "Marching Along Together" as our float started moving down the street to the completion of the parade route.

We were told by members of the Church that as the choir sang along the parade route, a warm glow of light radiated about our float and the choir. People were still bitter cold along the parade route, but sitting on the float in concert dress, coats off, we were warm, as our singing was being televised to the people of the nation.

The choir left for the airport as firework displays began shooting off. We always miss the fireworks, but we had accomplished more than momentary pleasure. We left a lasting memory.

Four years later the choir was invited back to sing for President Reagan's second inauguration. The First Presidency had given their permission, but things were just not right. Choir President Wendell Smoot said he felt something was amiss as he prayed about the choir going to Washington again. For one thing, adequate stage room had not been provided by the prominent Hollywood performer in charge of the program. But even that was not it. President Smoot felt strongly impressed that the choir should not go to Washington. The First Presidency told Brother Smoot that if he felt it best for the choir not to participate in the inauguration this time, they would support him in his decision. We did not go.

As it turned out, Washington was bitter cold at inauguration time. The inaugural parade and many activities were canceled. President Reagan was inaugurated in the White House. If the choir had gone, we would not have sung.

The Lord moves in a mysterious way, his wonders to perform.

At the inauguration of President George Bush, I was watching the proceedings with interest from my front room sofa where I lay recuperating from an operation—reliving the thrill of singing with the choir.

Remembering!

Mexico: Music Breaks the Language Barrier

Deplaning in Mexico City July 25, 1968, choir members heard strains of Spanish music played by a mariachi band in full dress. Banners waved "Welcome Mormon Tabernacle Choir." Smiling people threw arms around us—tears in their eyes and ours. What a joyful welcome.

Large banners in Spanish were attached to the side of school buses reading "Mormon Tabernacle Choir." They were waiting to transport the choir to Benemerito de las Amirico, our church-owned school. Students had been given a vacation for the week. We were to stay in their 12 student housing units.

Only one incident marred our arrival in Mexico City. A choir member, mistaking a window for a door at the airport, walked into a glass window. Glass shattered over him. Badly cut in the face and body, choir doctors gave him emergency treatment. He was then taken to the hospital and put under care of doctors from Mexico City, where he remained for the balance of the trip. Doctors, nurses and dentists, who are also singers in the choir, willingly give emergency care to choir members until local physicians arrive, but they are not licensed to practice medicine away from home.

While flying to Mexico, we stopped in San Antonio, Texas to perform at the World's Fair. We also sang at Lackland Military Training Center.

In Mexico City, concerts were scheduled to be sung at the Palace of Fine Arts. They were to be part of the International Festival of Arts being presented as "Cultural Olympics XIX."

Our host, Senor Ramon Noble, Director Of Music in the National Ministry of Culture of Mexico was delighted to have the choir in Mexico. We were also asked to participate in the dedication of our church-owned school complex.

The Mexican National Television Network had arranged to produce a TV special of the choir. Part of the special was to be shot at the Pyramid of the Sun and Moon. The rest would be filmed during concerts in the Palace of Fine Arts.

Before our first concert at the Palace of Fine Arts, demonstrators were thick around the concert hall. Streets filled for several blocks with unfriendly people carrying signs. Demonstration marchers, not focusing against the choir but against Americans in general, yelled, "Americans go home!" We left our buses to wade through the mob to the concert hall on the opposite side of the street. It was frightening.

After, the ladies changed into long white dresses, and men in black suits,white shirts, and black bow ties. Having a spare minute, we stopped to talk—regaining our composure.

Under the direction of Richard P. Condie and with Alexander Schreiner at the piano, the choir sang to an enthusiastic, jam-packed audience. Of course, "Battle Hymn" always brings our audience to their feet shouting and clapping, "More, more."

On the lighter side, after the concert a few choir members decided to go by subway to see the sights of Mexico City. Many friends in the choir are returned missionaries who speak foreign languages and know foreign subway systems. They make it easy to move about an unfamiliar city.

Traveling by subway we came to Mariachi Square. Bands were playing on all corners of the square. After listening for a while, we asked a band to play one of the songs we had sung in Spanish at our concert. We wanted to sing with them. A group of

Spanish teenagers, overhearing our conversation said, "You are not from the Mormon Tabernacle Choir. We just heard their concert. They sang like heavenly angels all dressed in white—and you are not angels." We smiled, explaining our presence on the square and that we were truly from the choir, but that we were just ordinary people blessed with a special musical talent. Singing as they listened, we were humbled by their comments.

A very simple and beautiful event, not scheduled, is my most endearing memory of my first trip to Mexico City. President N. Eldon Tanner was to dedicate the church school, the choir was to sing and Richard L. Evans, the choir's "Spoken Word," would address the audience.

After introductions and prayer, Elder Evans was speaking to the audience with the help of an interpreter. We were all listening intently, when the auditorium plunged into darkness from an electrical failure. We waited in the dark. A few moments later, we heard at the back of the audience, the faint sounds of "Lead Kindly Light" being sung in Spanish. The song increased in volume as others joined in. Part of the choir, including myself, began singing in English. Spontaneously, everyone burst into song. Then someone started to sing, "Come, Come Ye Saints" and we all joined in. We sang several hymns together, the audience in Spanish and the choir in English.

As lights turned on a half-hour later, there was not a dry eye. Tears were on the faces of everyone. A great feeling of love and fellowship radiated back and forth between choir and congregation as we wiped eyes and smiled at each other.

Elder Evans then stood up and continued his talk; Brother Condie directed the choir in concert; and President Tanner spoke, finishing with the dedicatory prayer.

After the dedication, the choir went outside to board buses. We found many of our audience waiting. These beautiful Mexican people smiled, hugged, and cried with us—communicating innermost feelings. Music had broken the language barrier.

Later at the stake center, dinner and a program were prepared for the choir by our Mexican hosts. On the program they danced and sang numbers from their latest stake dance and music festival. They were excited about performing for the choir and happy when the choir thanked them by singing.

The love and friendship of these beautiful Mexican people still remains vivid in my memory.

An incident happened as the choir left Mexico for the United States. We had been sent to two different concourses waiting for planes to arrive. I was visiting with friends when a man came up and asked where he could find our choir president, Ike Stewart. We directed him to the other concourse. Later, I saw the man again and commented to my friend, "Look, isn't that the man who was looking for President Stewart? He must not have found him after all."

Boarding our plane, we didn't think any more about it until we heard a commotion behind our seat. Airline personnel were removing someone from our plane—to my surprise, it was the man we had spoken to on the concourse. He had attempted to stow away, and would have succeeded except for one fatal mistake—he lit up a cigarette.

My friends and I have laughed about our "stow away" many times. He should have known better than to light up a cigarette on a choir plane.

Those were pre-highjacking days when planes were comparatively safe in the air. Now tight security is exercised whenever we travel. Boarding passes are required of all choir members and a careful roll-call is taken.

For our second trip to Mexico City in August 1972, the choir was invited to sing at an LDS area conference. Our contract with the Mexican Government specified the choir sing several songs at the conference. Concerts were to be given and we were to record three songs in Spanish in the auditorium or the conference could not be held. It had to be termed as a "Cultural Event," not a religious service. (We were allowed to record four songs in Spanish for the record album in Salt Lake before we left and three when we returned home, but three songs were to be recorded at the conference auditorium.)

President Harold B. Lee and several General Authorities flew on the planes with the choir to Mexico City. President Lee gave a special prayer over the microphone on the plane and blessed the choir. He asked the Lord to take care of our families while we were away from home, that we would have a safe trip and do the Lord's work.

The choir arrived again in Mexico to a very friendly welcome. Buses were waiting to take us to our hotel and then on to the National Auditorium to set the stage and sound for conference.

President Ike Stewart introduced Senor Ramon Noble to the choir. Senor Noble enthusiastically greeted us, happy we were going to sing the songs he had arranged in the Spanish language.

Before conference the next day, the choir broadcast "Music And The Spoken Word" to the world, with Richard P. Condie directing, Alexander Schreiner at the organ and Richard L. Evans giving the spoken word. Conference began, with President Harold B. Lee presiding.

Over 15,000 saints in attendance were uplifted by the spiritual messages of the General Authorities. Two talks, given by local saints, were heart-warming. An elderly lady told of being visited 50 years ago by three men. She was instructed to watch for two missionaries who would come later, teaching the Gospel of Jesus Christ. It would be the true church. Five years later, two young men knocked at her door. Recognizing them as the young men she was to watch for, she listened to their gospel teachings and was baptized.

The other talk told the story of an investigator who wanted to know if the Book of Mormon was true. Missionaries taught him, encouraged him to pray, and promised he would find his answer. After the missionaries left, the man prayed. That night he dreamed of a road with seven paths leading away from it. Up ahead on one path stood a man beckoning to him, saying, "My name is David O. McKay. Follow me. The road I go is the right way." The next morning the investigator told the missionaries his dream. One missionary said, "Wait a moment," and left the room. He come back with a picture in his hand. His investigator saw it and immediately said, "Yes, yes, that is the man in my dream!" The picture was of President David O. McKay.

President Lee admonished the saints to live the commandments and stay close to their teachings as the adversary was loose for the last time. He gave the congregation many words of advice and counsel and also made the statement, "There will soon be more members of the church in South America than in the United States."

Traveling to the pyramids on Monday, the choir recorded part of the program for the Mexican National T.V. Network. On the way back we stopped at the church-owned school for lunch.

It was the one the choir had helped dedicate on its previous visit to Mexico. After lunch our buses moved on to the National Auditorium where we were to record our required three songs in Spanish. But a mixup in scheduling had occurred. Only one-half hour remained of the time allotted for the recording session.

Realizing the lateness of the choir, Senor Noble and several catholic priests were already setting up chairs for the choir. We quickly took our places—concerned! We knew we had never sung the three newly-arranged songs written in Spanish. They were completely new to us. We prayed to our Father in Heaven for help. Brother Condie had the choir read a song through once, just saying the Spanish words. The next time we sang music to the words. On the third time through, our music was recorded.

It was incredible. We recorded three songs in Spanish in one-half hour. Music we had never seen before. (I do remember how easily the words and music came to my mind. My thinking was clear. I found no difficulty in interpreting the written page.)

After the three songs were recorded, our technicians and the Spanish recording company rushed out of the booth, a look of awe on their faces. "Your songs were beautiful," they told us. "The Spanish diction was perfect!"

Back in the United States, the choir still had three more songs to record in Spanish before completing the record album. It took four difficult hours to record those last three songs.

"Cielito Lindo" is one of my most treasured choir recordings. It bears testimony that the Lord hears and answers our prayers. As I listen to the music of this record, I remember the Lord's blessing upon the choir to fulfill our commitment to the Mexican government.

The Mexican officials were impressed by the conference, the choir, and the culture it brought to Mexico. Some of our bus drivers said they would gladly give their life for any member of the choir. They were so grateful for making it possible to hear the words of our prophet. Our hotel manager, amazed at a group who did not smoke or drink, said, "The choir was very friendly, sincerely themselves, so easy to know and become friends."

Mission accomplished, we remembered President Harold B. Lee's words to the choir "Sing your hearts out. Live by the spirit, and teach by the spirit."

Brazil

For weeks I quietly pondered whether to accompany the choir to Brazil the last part of May 1981. My son Keith would be graduating from high school and it would also be my son Kay's birthday during the time I would be gone. What should I do? Being set apart as a missionary gave me a feeling of obligation to fulfil the commitment to my calling. But as a mother, my place was at my son's graduation. One evening I told Keith, "I'm not going to Brazil. I'll be at your graduation." But Keith said, "Mom, you're a missionary—you must go. If you were just going on a trip it would be different, but the choir is doing missionary work and I feel you should go to Brazil. Don't worry about things here at home. It will be OK and I love you." He held me, let me cry a little on his shoulder, then with tears in both our eyes, he again said, "It will be OK mom."

As planes touched down in Brazil, another enthusiastic, welcoming crowd greeted the choir. Saints were so excited to have the choir in Brazil. Again, language was not a barrier. We could feel and see the spirit of the people. The choir was to sing "Music for the Americas," at the festival to help the abandoned children of Brazil.

Arriving on the temple grounds in San Paulo, it had been arranged for the choir to stay in a newly-constructed complex of apartments, built so new missionaries and Brazilian families coming from long distances to the temple would have a place to sleep. It was all *new*. Towels and sheets had never been used. The choir was the first to stay in the new complex. Such a beautiful gesture, to let the choir be the first group to use their new facilities.

Part of the time we ate in the recreation hall of the church on the temple grounds, but on the first night dinner was served in a hotel ballroom. Afterwards, our hosts ushered the choir into another large room where a program had been planned to welcome us to Brazil. Interpreters at their sides, those in charge were able to communicate with us.

Most touching was an original song, sung by a new convert to the church. She had written about her conversion and accompanied herself on a guitar. Singing in Portuguese, she gave a more moving performance than I have ever witnessed. Her words were unfamiliar, but her expressions, tears, and singing, with such firm conviction, could not be misunderstood. By the time she finished, we all had tears in our eyes and knew the joy of her conversion. Music, the universal language, again crossed language barriers, reaching our hearts.

The next day, Sunday, nine ladies in a group outside on the temple grounds were trying to figure out how to go with a friend to a Brazilian ward. Having been a former missionary in Brazil, the friend had been invited to sing at a sacrament meeting. A member of a mission presidency found out our dilemma and offered to take us in his van.

Arriving at the chapel just eight minutes before the meeting, we received friendly greetings from the saints outside. Missionaries found out who we were and introduced us to the bishop. He immediately said, "Oh, you must all sing. Our people would be very disappointed to know you were here and didn't sing for us." Entering the chapel, we saw another member of the choir meeting friends from her son's mission. She also joined our group. We quickly decided to sing the ladies' trio arrangement of "Lift Thine Eyes" in the hymn book. Two missionaries handed us their English pocket hymnals and one of our group used a

Portuguese hymn book to accompany us. Our friend also sang her solo.

During the meeting we listened to the musical sounds of Portuguese as familiar sacrament prayers were spoken. Even though we could not speak their language, the expressions and actions of the speakers and the response of the saints reached our hearts. We knew and could feel their testimonies given with conviction from their hearts.

As we came down the aisle after church, we were embraced and loved. We were asked to autograph lesson manuals and ward programs by Saints wanting to keep a memory of our visit. They were so joyful at having members of the choir attend their sacrament meeting. And our joy was as great as theirs, for they had shared their love and testimonies with us.

Later, we attended our own choir sacrament and testimony meeting. Choir members expressed their feelings, telling experiences, and of their love for the Brazilian people—greatful for the opportunity to sing and help the abandoned children of Brazil.

After sacrament meeting we changed into concert clothes. We were scheduled to sing at the opening ceremonies of the "Music for the Americas" festival. Its main purpose was to draw attention to, and raise funds for, the abandoned children of Brazil. They number in the millions. Many are preschool age. If the response of the people in our audience was any indication, our purpose in coming to Brazil was successful. People in our audience jumped to their feet as the last note of our concert was sung, clapping hard, calling, "More! More! Bravo!"

Of course choir life is not all work and no play. Three of my friends and I called a taxi. We planned to shop in San Paulo. After entering our taxi, we said "Mormon Tabernacle Choir" in our conversation. Our taxi driver became so excited I thought we were going to wreck. He said, "Mo-mom" and pointed to himself. Then began a conversation in pantomime. Rocking arms and holding up fingers, we were able to tell each other how many children in our families. The driver pointed to a building and said, "Kimball" and put his hands in a sleeping position, then "Tanner," and expressed a sad face and sickness. We learned many things about each other as we traveled downtown.

Our driver, so happy to have us as passengers in his taxi—how could we properly say goodbye to him, let him know we loved him and wished him well? I said, "I know, let's sing 'God Be With You 'Til We Meet Again'." As we sang, our driver joined in, singing in Portuguese.

We gave his shoulders a squeeze as we stepped out of his taxi, happy tears in all our eyes. We waved goodbye to our new Mormon friend from Brazil.

On Tuesday, the choir traveled to the resort town of Guaruja After eating a banquet, we had a great romp on the beach, wading in the breakers of the ocean. We were teasing Jerry and JoAnn Ottley. Jerry had a cold and JoAnn hurt her foot, so we called them "Shuffles and Snuffles."

Later in the afternoon the choir arrived back in San Paulo to sing our final concert. When the concert was completed, we began to sing encore numbers. To our surprise, saints in the audience unrolled a long paper sign with large letters. It read "We Love You!" We began singing "Battle Hymn of the Republic." (Have you ever tried singing with tears in your eyes and a lump in your throat?) We ended by singing with real feeling, "God Be With You 'Til We Meet Again."

Going back on our buses to the temple grounds was a happy time. Many Saints staying at the temple complex boarded our buses, too. They sat in the extra seats, or stood in the aisles. Men of the choir gave up their seats, and stood for the ride back to the temple grounds. Brazilian Saints had traveled great distances to attend temple sessions to have their families sealed and to also hear the choir. Some sold all their possessions for this privilege. They were so happy, just to be with us. One of the choir members near me could speak German, a Brazilian husband could speak German and his wife Portuguese. By means of a three-way translation, we learned of their joy and sacrifice coming to the temple to be sealed and how they felt about being with the choir and hearing us sing. We had many such experiences on the buses as we traveled to and from our destinations. We were able to rejoice with these saints, share in their stories of conversion and their feelings of being sealed in the house of the Lord.

When we arrived back at the temple grounds, an extemporaneous program was held in the recreation hall of the our Church. Everyone took turns performing—choir members, Brazilian saints, missionaries alike, all offering to taking part. Quoting from my journal, "It was a super and great experience, but the highlight of the evening happened when a Brazilian, who had only been a member of the Church for one month, was tuning his guitar, preparing to sing."

"A missionary stood and told the choir the story of this man's conversion to the Church. He was a Baptist minister. One day he happened to see and read a pamphlet telling the beliefs of our Church. He told his wife he had been searching for the truth but was unable to find the answers to his questions. After reading the pamphlet, his questions were answered. Locating our missionaries, he invited them to his home and told them he wanted to be baptized the next day. The missionaries quickly gave him all the discussions and he was baptized. The missionaries said, "The Baptist minister was an 'Instant Mormon'. He knew more about the scriptures than they did. He had the Book of Mormon, Pearl of Great Price, and Doctrine and covenants read in two days."

"As this former Baptist minister sang and played for us, it became evident he was a professional. Tears slid down our faces as we listened to him play and thought of his conversion. He received several encores."

We went back to our rooms, packed bags, and slept for three hours. We ate breakfast at 6:00 a.m., then boarded buses to go to the airport. Brazilian saints stood on all sides saying goodbye, waving and singing, "God Be With You 'Til We Meet Again." We looked back and watched until the people and the temple disappeared from sight.

Landing in Dallas, Texas to go through customs I was thinking about home: my heart was heavy, it was time for Keith's graduation exercises. I found a corner by myself and had a good cry. Seeing tears on my face, my friends put comforting arms around me. It was difficult to be in Dallas and know my boy was walking across the stage at the high school receiving his diploma.

When we arrived at the Salt Lake Airport, Keith and his date were waiting with our family. They had left their graduation dance to meet the plane. Keith threw his arms around me. We stood for a long time just holding each other tight and crying on each other's shoulder: then I turned to the rest of my family, who were waiting with open, arms. I gave Keith another hug, and sent him back to his graduation dance.

Brazil was a time of sharing and giving: helping the abandoned children and singing to non-members who wanted to know more about the Mormons and the Tabernacle Choir. The choir left Brazil with a great love for its people and their traditions, and with fortified testimonies filling our hearts.

European Tour

President Harold B. Lee visited the choir on January 25th, 1973 and invited us to sing for an area conference to be held in Munich, Germany in August. Included in the proposed trip to Munich were stops to sing in Paris and London. In London, we would make television recordings for the BBC and also record the *Messiah* with the Royal Philharmonic Orchestra.

German television producer Lutz Wellnitz requested to film a television special on the choir. Extensive arrangements were made to film a television special in Europe and Utah, to be telecast throughout Europe at a later date.

For our tour, two new ladies' formals—one blue and the other white—were added to our wardrobe. The men also had new suits to match.

Choir planes taking off from the Salt Lake Airport were scheduled to refuel in Bangor, Maine. Kurt and I called home when we arrived there, checking on our children before leaving the States.

Mother and the children told us that a skunk had just visited our backyard where the children had been sleeping out on the grass in sleeping bags. It sprayed over everything. With desperation in their voices, they asked what to do about the smell all over them and the sleeping bags.

Dr. Merrill Wilson, a member of the choir standing close by, overheard our problem at home. He suggested washing everything affected by skunk odor with tomato juice—it would kill the odor. We told the children to open several cans of tomato juice, douse themselves and the sleeping bags, and to keep scrubbing until the smell was gone. We told them, "Go to it—good luck—we love you and grandma will show you how."

Mother was grateful for the help. She had been at a loss, not knowing what to do.

Our emergency taken care of, we settled down with the rest of the choir personnel for a long flight over the Atlantic Ocean.

After the lights were out inside the plane, harmonica music began playing. Merrill Wilson, the doctor in charge of our plane, tried to find the source of the music to obtain quiet so everyone could sleep. He walked up and down the aisles, but to no avail. Catchy tunes floated through the air, nice to listen to, but disturbing to some. Merrill gave up, sat down in his plane seat and the music soon ceased and quiet prevailed. We later found out that Lynn Allen had an inch long harmonica inside his mouth that he had been playing. What a bunch—there is always a joker in every crowd.

Arriving in Germany, we received an enthusiastic greeting from the German people who were delighted the choir was to be part of their area conference. As our hotels were not ready, buses took the choir directly to the Olympic Sports Hall where we were to set the stage and rehearse for conference. Given a chance to relax, the choir members stretched out anywhere they could find a spot, even putting three plastic chairs with raised edges together.

Sharp-edged chairs soon bit into our sides, so we left for a stroll through the hall corridors. My, what a sight—people suffering from jet lag sprawled out in every available space. In one place, three people were lying flat on their backs on three tables, arms folded across their chests, fast asleep, looking like they were ready for the morgue. We all had a good chuckle over it.

With relaxing time over, the call came to rehearse. Richard Condie and Choir President Ike Stewart gave instructions, set the stage and then rehearsed the choir in songs for conference.

After rehearsal, our hotels were ready. We crashed into bed, grateful for a chance to rest.

Lutz Wellnitz and his television crew began filming the choir in the Olympic Stadium the next morning for his TV special. From the Olympic Stadium, we moved to King Ludwig's castle in the Bavarian Alps for additional filming. These were long, tiring sessions—standing in one spot. Each session took hours, but the end result was worthwhile.

Our next film site and concert was held on the stage of the Passion Playhouse in Oberammergau. Everyone in Oberammergau is involved in the production of the Passion Play, held every ten years, which tells the life of Christ. Audiences travel from all over the world to see the play. To the townspeople, the Passion Play and its theater are very special and sacred. But for the first time since the stage was built over 100 years ago, they were allowing someone else to use their stage. It gave us a feeling of oneness with the people of Oberammergau.

Filled with emotion after the Tabernacle Choir concert, the people of Oberammergau extended a warm invitation for the choir to return again, glad to share their special stage with the choir. Oberammergau has become a cherished memory.

The next day, excitement ran throughout the choir in anticipation of singing for the Munich conference. Five languages—German, French, Italian, Spanish, and English— were spoken in the audience. Through interpreters each person heard conference by means of a small transistor radio tuned into the language of their choice. Everyone—except members of the choir—had a small radio.

The audience singing "Let Us Oft Speak Kind Words to Each Other" (each person in their own language), brought tears to all our eyes. Later, the choir sang "Come, Come Ye Saints" in four languages, each verse in a different language.

General Authorities of the Church spoke, giving love and counsel to the people. Several talks were in English, but Saints who were asked to speak, spoke in their own language. The choir, listening to sincere testimonies of Church members speaking in different languages, felt a special spirit. We could not understand their words, but the expressions on their faces, their body language and the sincerity of each voice conveyed the message of their love and understanding of the gospel.

President Lee spoke, commending the choir for their ability to sing in several languages and thanked us for sharing our music with the saints. He then taught the people. Concluding, he said, "Peace be with you. Not the peace that comes from legislation in the halls of congress, but the peace that comes in the way that the Master said, by overcoming all the things of the world. That God may help us so to understand, and may you know that *I know with a certainty that defies all doubt that this is His work*, that He is guiding and directing us today as He has done in every dispensation of the gospel, and I say that with the humility of my soul, in the name of Jesus Christ, Amen."

Meeting and talking with Church members after conference, we learned the content of talks we had heard in foreign languages—of inspirational events and sincere testimonies borne. Local choirs furnished music for the afternoon session of conference and since all available seats were taken, choir members were not able to attend. So we prevailed upon our bus drivers to take us over the border to Salzburg, Austria, so we could see where the *Sound of Music* was filmed.

In the meantime, some of our choir group were ahead of us. They rented two cars so they could go to a missionary conference. They also planned to go to Salzburg, stopping occasionally, to see historic spots along the way.

In Rothenburg they were told of a historic house often photographed by tourists. The choir members walked, and after a time found the house leaning against an old town wall. They knocked on a door. No one answered. They were about to leave when a sweet older lady leaned out of an upper window. She told them the house was closed, but asked if they wanted anything else. Speaking in English, the choir members replied, "We are from the United States, traveling from Salt Lake City, Utah to sing with the Mormon Tabernacle Choir in Munich." Instantly the woman's countenance changed. She excitedly told them to wait while she came down to open the door. Overjoyed, she told them she was a member of the Church and had been very disappointed she could not attend the conference in Munich. She said it had been a very long time since she had seen any Church members or partaken of the sacrament as she lived so far away from a branch of the Church.

After touring the little house and getting better acquainted, they decided to hold a meeting in her front room. Songs learned by the choir for conference were sung by the choir members, reports given of the conference message, and testimonies borne. Everyone in the room new the Lord had led them to this dear member of the Church who was unable to attend conference.

Monday morning the choir had an early rehearsal for our open air concert in Marianplatz Square. We were taken early to the shopping center to browse and shop before the concert.

While shopping, several choir members were recognized by Saints from behind the Iron Curtain who had attended the conference. Delighted to have an opportunity to visit, they told how they had been granted permission to attend conference, but with one stipulation—a member of each family would be left behind to insure that those going to conference would return. They were unable to bring luggage or extra money—but were allowed to wear just the clothes on their back.

Talking to them further, we learned of their need for clothing behind the Iron Curtain. Sweaters, dresses, shirts, pants, and other items were purchased by choir members, and a plan was devised. The Saints from behind the Iron Curtain would wear several sets of clothes home—three shirts, double sweaters, two or three pairs of pants, etc. They would be hot, but it was worth it to be able to take new clothing back to their families.

While we were shopping, television crews set up cameras to take their last shots of the choir in Germany. We gathered to sing in the square in front of the town hall. Kurt stood among the people watching, close to a blind man. The man asked what was happening. He could feel something special in the air. When he found out it was the Mormon Tabernacle Choir preparing to sing a concert, tears ran down the blind man's face. He told Kurt he was a member of the Church and had traveled from a neighboring town. He was overjoyed at being able to hear the choir again.

When the filming was completed, the choir walked two blocks to the railway station to board trains for Paris, France. German members of the church met us at the train station expressing their love and thanks for singing at their conference.

Our missionary work completed, we left clean, beautiful Germany with its windows full of flowers. We also left feeling a strong love for its people.

In Paris, missionaries and members of the Church greeted the choir enthusiastically as we left our train and moved to the buses. We sang a very successful concert in Lourve Court, but we were disappointed to find the only day the Lourve is closed to the public was Tuesday, the day of our concert. But our purpose in coming to France was to open doors for the missionaries and our audience consisted mostly of non-members and investigators of the Church. They were obviously impressed and moved by our music, because some in our audience contacted our missionaries, who then taught them the gospel.

The choir flew to England to tape a Christmas television special for the BBC to be shown throughout Europe. We were to also give a concert in Prince Albert Hall, and the next day to record the *Messiah* with the Royal Philharmonic Orchestra.

Central Hall was decorated for Christmas this very hot day in July. Members of the Military Guard Bands of London were ready to rehearse with the choir for our Christmas TV special. As rehearsal progressed, we all knew we had a problem. The synchronization between the choir and the band was completely out of balance—we were not singing and playing together. There was real cause for concern. By the time our short rehearsal ended, the problem still had not been solved. Murmuring began to be heard among the choir and the band.

As we moved into a hall where a light lunch had been prepared, words of discord were heard everywhere. I had never heard such dissension among choir members before—trying to lay blame. I felt like jumping on a chair and saying, "Stop, it's not the Lord's way, but someone else creating dissension among us."

After lunch the choir and band took their places back on stage. The hall was packed, not a seat available anywhere. Many guests had been invited for the taping the choir's Christmas special.

Last minute preparations were being made by the technical crew before the cameras rolled. Waiting in place, a wonderful, thinking member of the choir passed notes through the choir. Each note read the same, "The pioneers did it and so can we. Pray with faith." It woke us up. Even though the prayer had been said earlier, silent prayers were uttered in our hearts for a good performance. From the first downbeat our music was in perfect unison, with choir and band performing with precision. We knew the Lord had heard and answered our prayers.

The next night, Prince Albert Hall was filled to capacity. We sang to an enthusiastic audience, which paid tribute to our performance with shouts of "Bravo, bravo, more, more."

The choir's recording session for the *Messiah* took place at Kingsway Hall with the Royal Philharmonic Orchestra. Everything went smoothly, and we cut a beautiful record.

Just before the last session of recording, we had a bomb threat at the hotel where choir members were staying. The day before, extensive damage by a bomb had been reported at another hotel close by. With apprehension, choir members hurriedly packed suitcases, put them outside the hotel to be picked up by trucks, and walked to our final recording session at Kingsway Hall.

As planes took off for the United States, we looked back at the coastline of England with a feeling of satisfaction for a job well done. Missionary work would go forward.

Toward the end of our flight, Kurt and I were looking out our window when a bolt of lightning hit our plane. There was a big flash of light and the plane jolted. A moment later the phone blinked for the stewardess. As she listened, her eyes became big as saucers when she heard over the phone from the captain that our plane had just been hit by lightning. Thank goodness for modern technology and new equipment installed on our plane to withstand a lightning bolt.

Returning to Utah, Lutz Wellnitz and his TV crews continued to film the choir in many locations throughout the state in order to finish his television special. Our first location was to be on the salt flats west of the Great Salt Lake. TV crews flew above us in a helicopter. The choir walked on the salt flats singing. Segments were filmed at the Tabernacle, "This is the Place Monument," Arches National Monument, and Snowbird Ski Resort.

We were all very hot as we walked on the salt flats, and the coldest I have every been in my life was on top of the mountain at Snowbird. Coats were off when actual TV scenes were shot, with icy wind whistling around us. But the end result was worth it and a great television show completed. Wellnitz flew back to Germany to cut and splice his film into a polished program to be seen later throughout Europe.

In a letter to Ike Stewart, president of the choir at that time, Wellnitz wrote that his filming of the choir was the best program he had produced in his career.

Leaving the completed film at his studio, Wellnitz left for another assignment, but his plane never landed. It crashed and Lutz Wellnitz was killed in November, 1973. His work lives on in his television special of the choir.

Here are some excerpts from letters received by the choir after this tour:

—Today at the eve of Christmas I heard your choir on German TV. It was, for me, one of the most beautiful programs of this year. Thank you very much.

—One day before Christmas we heard the Mormon Tabernacle Choir on television here in Bavaria. This was a real Christmas gift to me and my family. Never before have I heard a choir singing in that way your choir did; it was a music so alive and seemed to me as if the music and the country was one thing. It was real grand. Thank you so much. So best of luck to you and your choir and thanks for music that brought to us a big joy.

—The finest gift to Christmas I received yesterday by the German television your famous "Salt Lake Mormon Tabernakle (sic) Chorus" sang songs of your home, Mozart's Ave Maria, and the Pilgrim Chorus of Wagner in a quality I never heard formerly. Thank you, thank you all singer together for this gift. If I had the money to visit you in Salt Lake tomorrow I would start to thank you personally! I like your home-country and I am full of wonder about the native country of the Mormons with the mountains and the Grand Canyon, but only by pictures. Please, thank in my name each of your singers for this wonderful gift and tell them, the day will come—maybe in a few years, that I have enough to visit you in Utah—and then I am able to thank you personally.

—We were told in meetings here for the last month that there would be a broadcast of the Tabernacle Choir televised and so, informed all our members (active and inactive), as well as our investigators and teaching contacts of the program. We weren't quite sure what it would be, thinking that only a portion of the program would deal with the choir. But, were so pleased to find the entire hour-long program was about the choir, the country in Utah, and the performances in Europe.

I want you to realize what a spiritual boost this is to these people. It is a trial every day of their lives to simply be a member of the Mormon church. But when we hear the choir sing and see what the Church really is, then it just makes it easier to "keep on keepin' on."

These people were so grateful for the conference in Munchen [Munich]. They never let a Sunday go by without remembering it. You can imagine what an impact a broadcast would have on these little groups. Actually letting them know they are a part of a growing concern: and what a wonderful symbol and mascot of our faith the Mormon Tabernacle Choir is here in Europe. It gets us into many homes, simply because of the sincere message the choir always exemplifies. The choir simply sings what they are.

President Harold B. Lee sent a letter to the choir after the Munich conference. He wrote,

We are mindful that your service does not come without personal sacrifice, both by choir members and your families. Through your work...countless lives have been and will be lifted. Testimonies have been and will be strengthened. The work of the Lord has been and will be given further motivation.

Scandinavia and Europe:
Music Reaches the Heart

Weeks before the final sign-up for the choir's tour to Scandinavia and European countries in June 1982, Kurt and I had a difficult decision to make. Our boy Keith and our girl Susan were both talking of going on missions at the same time as the choir tour. We all felt missions were first priority. Our family budget would be strained to the limit if Kurt went on the tour, while we sent two missionaries into the field.

Many of our ancestors had emigrated from Norway, Denmark, and England. Arrangements had already been made to have my non-member relatives as guests for the choir concert in Aalborg, Denmark. We hoped Kurt could be with them to answer questions about the choir and our church. We also had a strong desire to visit the land of our ancestors.

Tour cost for a choir member is paid out of choir funds, but spouses pay individually, four months before a trip.

We fasted and prayed for an answer. By coincidence, it was the same day we went to renew our temple recommends. After signing recommends, we visited with our bishop, discussing whether Kurt should go with me or stay home. The bishop left the decision on our own shoulders.

Upon arrival at the stake president's house, Kurt and I sat in our car talking. We had almost decided it was best for Kurt to stay home and not go to Scandinavia.

We went in to be interviewed by our stake president, Randy Benson. He signed our recommends and then we told him about fasting and praying, and why. President Benson talked with us for a few minutes, and we again had almost come to the conclusion Kurt should not go. Then President Benson was impressed that we should kneel down and pray to Heavenly Father for guidance. At the conclusion of President Benson's prayer, while we were still on our knees, with tears in his eyes President Benson said, "Kurt, you can go. The Lord is making this a test of your faith." We all had tears in our eyes as we arose from our knees with a sure knowledge things would work out for Kurt to go to Scandinavia.

An excerpt from my journal written before we left on choir tour reads:

I have felt there is something in Europe that we are to accomplish or the Lord would not be helping Kurt and me the way he has. Things have happened in a natural way to make this feeling more a reality. Money came to our door from unexpected sources from persons who had owed us money in the past, forgotten about it, but had finally remembered and paid us just in time for the trip.

But someone else must have known about our desire to go, because the day before we were to leave, one daughter was in the hospital in Tucson, a son fell and hurt himself, requiring emergency treatment, and our son-in-law enroute back to his home in Arizona stopped at our home and we took him for emergency care for severe back pain. Our family needed us. But our son Alan and his wife Terry said, "Dad and Mom—you go; we'll bring our children and stay at your house while you are gone. We will take care of everything. All will be well. Go and don't worry." Jerry Ottley has commented to the choir how so many things go wrong in the choir families just before a tour.

Things did work out. Our daughter, Susan met and became engaged to her future husband before we left for Europe. She made arrangements for a temple marriage instead of a mission.

My brother La Grand called from Wyoming asking if our son Keith could help him temporarily on an electrical job. Keith worked and earned all the money needed to buy his clothes, supplies, pay his plane fare and first two month's expenses for his mission. He entered the mission home on his nineteenth birthday, the same day choir planes lifted off for Europe.

Early in the morning we were preparing to take Keith to the mission home in Provo, Utah, and then travel back to Salt Lake Airport to catch our plane. We discovered the children needed $40.00 more to help with expenses at home. We gave it to them, but realized it was money we really needed elsewhere.

In Provo we picked up my mother to go with us to the mission home. Enroute she said, "I would like to help you on your tip to Europe; please let me give you $40.00 to add money for your trip." All the way through our tour we never wanted and the Lord blessed us in many ways.

Just before the choir left, President Gordon B. Hinckley came to the Tabernacle bidding the choir "Godspeed." He said, "Go with our blessings—blessings of all the General Authorities. We will pray for your safety in traveling and for the well-being of your families and children you leave behind."

Norway was the first stop on the choir's concert tour. Shortly after our arrival, choir members had free time to see the city of Bergen. A small group decided to go on a tram to see a view of the city, but somewhere along the route Kurt and I became separated from the group. Later, we saw three other choir members who said they were going up a tram and would we like to go with them. They felt they knew which bus to take and the direction to go.

Talking with our friends on the bus, we told them about our relatives in Denmark, how they planned to take us to dinner, and how, in turn, we would have them as our guests in Aalborg for our concert.

Out of all the choir members we could have met, this one choir member had the forethought to go to the Temple Square Visitor's Center before we left. She obtained pamphlets about our church in various languages of the countries we were to perform in. She offered her Danish tracts to me for my relatives in Aalborg, and she brought them to me at the afternoon rehearsal.

We continued on, taking the tram to the top of the mountain and saw a spectacular view of Bergen, Norway. Moving to another outlook, we saw another breathtaking view. We were awed at the beauty all around us. Overhearing our delighted comments about the surrounding area, a couple standing next to us spoke in hesitant English and asked where we were from. We told them of the choir's forthcoming concert at the Bergenhallen and of our tour. They introduced themselves, telling us they were native Norwegians enjoying the view of their city.

Visiting with them further, Kurt talked about his ancestors from Norway. In the conversation Kurt asked them specific question about the territory. (Doing his genealogy, Kurt had been stopped on his Norwegian line, not knowing where to look next for his ancestors.) To our surprise this couple knew the area Kurt was talking about—gave him the answers he needed to break the barrier and find the location of his ancestors from Norway. Kurt had been looking for a city or town, but he found that the name he had been looking for was not a town, but a suburb of a town close to Oslo not listed on a map. This was a red letter day for Kurt in his genealogical research.

It was interesting to note when we arrived back at our hotel and talked with our friends in the original group going to a tram, that they had taken a different tram on the other side of Bergen. By losing our way and taking another tram, Danish tracts were placed in our hands for my relatives and Kurt now knew the location of his Norwegian ancestors, giving him a breakthrough in his genealogical search.

The Tabernacle Choir, singing their first concert in Bergen that night to a full house, received the rare European handclap.

In the European concert world, concert goers have a special handclap for excellence, which has been heard very few times in any concert hall. Clapping begins normally, increasing in intensity to a high crescendo, then turns into a slow, rhythmic, even handclap. When this happens, a performer knows he has reached the heart of his audience. The Tabernacle Choir received the European handclap in every concert hall we performed in. We were told that in some of our concert halls as we moved from country to country, performers had only received the European handclap three or four times in the lifetime of the concert hall. It was exciting to listen to the change of sound in the handclap from the audience, as we now knew the meaning of the slow, even rhythm. Hearts touched, many investigators listened to the gospel message, and doors opened for our missionaries.

The choir sailed on the Greek ship "Oceanus." It was to serve as the choir's hotel for the next ten days. After a concert the choir was bused back to the ship. While we slept, the boat sailed to our next destination.

The next morning choir members met in the ship's lounge to rehearse three songs to be sung in the language of the next country we were to perform in. Our language coach helped the choir to enunciate words correctly and then Jerold Ottley led the choir, putting words and music together.

It was a fun time learning to sing songs in several languages. By the time our boat docked, the choir had learned the songs to be sung at our next concert. Our audiences loved hearing their favorite songs sung by the choir in their own language. It brought down the house. By the time we sang "Battle Hymn," the audience sprang to their feet shouting "Bravo"—clapping loud and long—then a change came, a rhythmic handclap that resounded in the concert hall. On several evenings the choir heard the European handclap four or five times during a concert. Exciting, to say the least.

The choir moved from Bergen, Norway to Stockholm, Sweden and then onto Helsinki, Finland. As we docked in Finland, the choir was in concert dress on the deck of the ship looking over the rails at the crowd gathered at the dock. There were many government officials, business dignitaries, and Saints. The choir sang "Finlandia" from the deck of the ship to the people below us. We then filed down the ship's ramp to the waiting people who formed a reception line. Choir members moved in a single line, being greeted and welcomed to Finland.

Many receptions were held and many honors bestowed upon the choir by government officials, business executives, civic leaders, television heads and other important people of each country visited during our tour.

A small group from the choir, calling themselves the "Vocal Dimension Quartet," performed at receptions where there was not room for the entire choir. One of these was a reception in honor of the Queen of Norway, hosted by Ambassador John Loeb, Jr. at his private residence. Two hundred guests, including ambassadors of several nations, heads of state and movie personalities were present.

Television specials of the choir were filmed by the countries we visited throughout our tour, thus making it possible for many more people to hear the choir who were unable to attend our concerts.

After the choir's concert in Copenhagen, Denmark at the Tivoli Gardens Concerthallen, we were just filing off stage at the end of our concert when three Books of Mormon in Danish were noticed on a table. Inquiring, we discovered that no one owned the books. A choir member placed a Danish Book of Mormon in my hands to give my relatives the next day at Aalborg. Inch by inch, brochures, a Book of Mormon, and even information about the customs of our relatives and been put into my hands to help us greet our relatives we had never seen before in Denmark. I had also brought choir records and a beautiful book about the choir to give to them when we packed for our trip.

As the ship docked a little late, Kurt and I just had time to catch a bus and meet our relatives, the Per Davidson family, at a pre-arranged meeting place. It was instant friendship. Conversation was easy, as Per and Tov's two children, Frank and Heidi, had learned English in the school system. Heidi also had a friend with her visiting from the States who could speak both English and Danish, interpreting for Per, Tov, and Sophia, the grandmother. After eating at a lovely Danish restaurant, we visited for a while, becoming better acquainted, telling many news items of relatives in Denmark and the United States.

That evening at the concert, Kurt sat in the audience with our people in Aalborghallen, while I sang with the choir on stage. Handclapping was thunderous, then changed to the European slow, rhythmic handclap. My people especially liked Joanne Ottley's two solos in the middle of the concert.

Meeting out in front of the concert hall before going to our ship, we gave our relatives the Danish brochures, Book of Mormon, records, and choir book. In return, the grandmother had made a beautiful cross-stitched bellringer to hang on our front door at Christmas time. Love, kisses, and hugs were being given to each other when our relatives were tapped on the shoulder and given anti-Mormon literature by the picketers who had been shipped in from the States and followed the choir, passing out anti-Mormon literature to our audiences after every concert.

There my relatives stood, with the Book of Mormon in one hand, and anti-Mormon literature in the other. The picketer said as he handed the literature to them, "Here, know the truth about these Mormons." But I said, "You mean part truth; we'll leave the real truth with them" and I promptly took the "anti" materials from my people and slapped them into my music folder.

The Davidsons accompanied us back to the ship and we were just in time to see Jerry Ottley and his wife. My relatives were elated to be able to talk to Jerry and JoAnn and express their feelings of how they had enjoyed the concert.

Boarding the ship, we went to the top deck to lean over the railings to wave goodbye to our relatives. Choir members by our side said, "Let's go: one, two, three, go: We love you Davidsons—goodbye." They heard us and waved back as our ship pulled up anchor to go to the Netherlands to sing our next concerts in Amsterdam and Rotterdam. Kurt and I knew without a doubt as we left Denmark that our relatives were meant to hear the gospel. Danish tracts and the Book of Mormon were literally placed in our hands to give them. As we did so, another group didn't want them to know the truth and placed anti-Mormon materials in their hands at the very same time—but we won!

At Rotterdam, the choir was to meet in rehearsal at De Hoelen Concert Hall to set the stage, but Jerry was missing a choir. Where were they? They were all lined up across the street at a Baskin-Robbins ice cream parlor. Rehearsal finally got underway, Jerry shaking his head at his delinquent choir that could not resist a little touch of home in a foreign land.

Again, our concert was sold out and an enthusiastic audience gave the European handclap.

Leaving Amsterdam and our floating hotel, the choir flew to London to sing our last concert in Prince Albert Hall. People were seated in every available space—the hall was packed. What a responsive audience, what a thrilling climax, what a great experience—our tour to Europe. After the concert, "Music and the Spoken Word" was broadcast live by satellite to the world.

With a job well done, the choir flew home. Again, the missionary work will go forth and many accept the gospel touched by the music of the choir.

At one of the concert halls a member of the Church told me that in the audience at that particular hall (which was smaller than some of the others the choir had performed in) about 300 Latter-day Saints were in attendance and 2,500 non-members. This was to be about the same ratio of all our concerts. Our audiences were mostly non-members. It was a thrill for the choir to be so well-received by the people of Europe.

Choir program booklets were passed out at concerts, which not only gave the program listed for the evening, but gave additional facts about the choir. The last two pages of the booklet contained questions and answers about the Church, how to contact missionaries, and the address of the local mission home.

After the tour, letters poured in. President Ben E. Lewis in London wrote,

> I sat next to two women at the concert who asked me about the choir because they had not heard about it. During the course of the afternoon, we had opportunity to get fairly well acquainted and by the time the program had finished, we had become good friends. Out of the discussion, we received an invitation to have our missionaries come and call upon these two women. I think that tells the story of how they, and all of us, felt about the choir presentation. Thank you very much.

A missionary returning home from his mission in Sweden received a letter from a girl he had taught while laboring there. He had taught her for some time, without success. In her letter she said she had attended one of the choir concerts in Stockholm. By the end of the concert she was ready for baptism, and is now a member of the Church.

President Gordon B. Hinckley visited the choir upon our return to Salt Lake City. He thanked us on behalf of all the Brethren for a successful trip to Northern Europe. "We are grateful that the Lord watched over you and protected you. There is no question but what you are the Lord's choir. You sing for him and he blesses your efforts."

The Lord Opens
the Door to the Orient

With the coastline of Japan in sight, Kurt spoke to me in low tones, remembering the last time he had seen Japan—in 1945 at the end of World War II. His aircraft carrier, the USS Roi, was part of Admiral Halsey's fleet, located about 175 miles from the coastline of Japan. Kurt, assigned as a radar operator, had taken navigational fixes on Mount Fuji.

Later, with the surrender signed, a great celebration began. Kurt saw the sky full of planes as far as the eye could see, in a huge victory flyover above the fleet and over Tokyo. Back home in the center of town, we were singing and dancing in the streets of Provo. The war was over.

Two months later, Kurt's aircraft carrier came back to the States for quick repair before sailing to the Pacific again, Kurt hurriedly called and told me to meet him at the Salt Lake train station Thursday night at 8:00 p.m. We traveled to Provo, and at 11:30 p.m. woke my parents to tell them we were going to be married the next day. Surprised, but knowing we had been engaged for over a year, Mom, Dad, and Kurt's mother helped us with fast arrangements that began at 6:00 a.m. the next morning when a store manager opened his store so I could select and buy a wedding dress. We then made a visit to our bishop and stake president for temple recommends, had wedding reception invitations printed, addressed and in the mail that same day, obtained blood tests, the marriage license, and just made the 5:00 p.m. session at the Salt Lake Temple—well almost. We were at the courthouse at 5:00 p.m. as the clerk was closing the door for the weekend. We prevailed on the clerk to stay and write out our marriage license, then hurried over to the temple where temple workers had held up the 5:00 p.m. session—knowing we were coming to be endowed and married. (During wartime, everyone was understanding and helpful to servicemen who had such limited time at home.) After we were married and came out of the temple, we didn't have a place to stay for the night, but finally, we found a hotel room.

Kurt and I spent Saturday seeing the tourist attractions in Salt Lake and Sunday morning decided to go to Temple Square where we heard our first live broadcast of the Mormon Tabernacle Choir. Beautiful music filled the Tabernacle. Little did Kurt and I realize the part the choir would play in our lives.

By Sunday afternoon we were back in Provo. Monday night our reception was held in the recreation hall of our ward. Kurt wore his Navy uniform and my friends wore pastel dresses. It was a lovely reception, but only one difficulty: Kurt's leave was about up. He would in fact be AWOL by three hours before he arrived back at his ship. (He was restricted to the ship and given scrub duty.)

Kurt was a radar operator for his ship, but he also served as the captain's jeep driver. When the captain came on board and found Kurt restricted, he was surprised and said, "What the...are YOU doing restricted to the ship?" After hearing Kurt's reasons, the captain had him call his new wife in Utah to come to San Fransisco. We had three more days together, then Kurt's ship sailed. I stood on the dock watching as his ship went under the Oakland Bay Bridge—destination, the Orient.

Now, the Mormon Tabernacle Choir, approaching the coastline of Japan in peace, was being welcomed by the people of Japan. (One good thing did come out of the terrible destruction of the war: it opened the door so the gospel could be taught.) Through song, the choir would reach the hearts of the Japanese people.

As the choir deplaned and cleared customs, Japanese Saints were in lines waving Japanese and American flags. Large banners were held up saying, "Welcome, Mormon Tabernacle Choir." Before boarding buses, each choir member was given a small bouquet of flowers, with a combination bow and a handshake. We all had tears in our eyes. This type of welcome continued all through our tour of Japan. Love and respect grew between the choir and the Japanese people as we toured form city to city.

Although our flights to Japan arrived five hours late, Hotel Otani prepared a nice lunch from our missed banquet. We were instructed to choose one of the hotel's many restaurants rather than eat together as a choir. While we were eating, we noticed a Japanese gentleman eating alone at the next table. Introducing ourselves to Herbert Mauayama we discovered that he had arrived a week before from his home in California to work out details with TV stations. He was not a member of the Church, but would be acting as interpreter and liaison officer between American and Japanese television for the choir's tour to Japan which was being sponsored by the Japanese television network NHK (Nippon Hoso Kyokai). The next day Herbert was introduced to the choir.

As we continued to visit with Herbert, Kurt mentioned what his thoughts had been as he approached the coastline of Japan. A deep and very interesting conversation ensued between them. Herbert, an American of Japanese descent, had been assigned to American intelligence during the war. He and Kurt spent more than an hour discussing their war experiences, McArthur's takeover of Japan, and the American occupation. A close bond developed between them. Herbert sought out Kurt throughout the tour, asking many questions about the Church and choir. Our friendship grew.

On Sunday, sacrament meeting was to be held; a fireside had been prepared by the Japanese Saints for the choir. Early Sunday morning I had the impression that we should invite Herbert to the sacrament service and fireside. I asked Kurt about calling on the phone to invite him, but Kurt felt we should not call—if we saw Herbert we should ask him. Feeling strong about inviting Herbert, I prayed to Heavenly Father to help us.

Two lines were forming for breakfast—one from one end of the table, and another from the other end. As we came to the center with our tray filled, Herbert was coming from the other end of the line. We sat down together and were given the golden opportunity to extend an invitation to Herbert to go with us to sacrament meeting. Being very busy with television schedules, Herbert was not sure he would be free. In fact, we had the impression that he would rather not. But in a few minutes he asked us when we would be back at the hotel before going to sacrament meeting and then said nothing more.

Later, as we arrived in the hotel lobby, there was Herbert waiting for us to go to sacrament meeting. During the meeting he asked many questions about the church, what the sacrament represented, and about our other beliefs.

From then on we shared many interesting times together. Herbert was uncertain how to entertain us. He was used to going to a hotel bar to drink and visit, but he found out that Kurt was fond of ice cream, so we would meet in the hotel cafe to eat ice cream and talk.

Herbert was the beginning of our missionary experience with the choir in Japan. Missionary work moved forward from the time our planes touched on Japanese soil until the choir left Japan, leaving doors open for our missionaries. Differences of language posed no barrier as audience after audience responded with great warmth.

After concerts, in the concert hall foyers, boxes were filled with referral cards deposited by our listeners, wanting to know more about the Church. Concerts were given in major Japanese cities to sellout audiences. As news spread of our concert tour, many persons were unable to obtain tickets, but Tabernacle Choir TV specials, broadcast all over Japan, were seen and heard by millions of viewers.

At a special buffet reception sponsored by NHK television, Chuukyo's President Shinnosuke Satoh, and KSL's J. Spencer Kinard signed a document declaring a sister-station relationship between the two TV stations, designed to lead to an exchange of video tapes. Mr Satoh said, "We have sown a seed and what beautiful flowers it will produce and what wonderful fruit it will bear depends on the efforts of both partners." Individual members of the choir were given a large pearl, encased in a square velvet box, as a token of appreciation.

Members and non-members followed the choir from concert to concert. In one audience Kurt sat by a non-member who told him he had attended every concert. The Japanese people were very gracious and receptive, ready to hear the gospel. Missionary work was performed individually and collectively. The choir was told about a Catholic priest who had been given the missionary discussions, was interested, but had decided against baptism. He felt he would lose his occupation. The missionaries invited him to our first concert, and when it was over the priest informed the missionaries he wanted to be baptized. He said he was impressed and moved by a special spirit radiating from the choir. He knew what the missionaries had taught him was true. Several of his congregation followed the priest into the waters of baptism.

On the bus after the choir's final concert, our bus driver announced on his microphone how he and his co-worker, a "cricket girl" (A cricket girl helps by signaling with a whistle to back up the bus, direct loading and unloading of passengers, and watch for tight traffic situations) had enjoyed our concert. The girl asked the driver to announce on the bus microphone that she would appreciate hearing the members of the choir sing again the Japanese folk song "The Little Dragonfly" we had sung that night. She desired to sing it with us. She silently bent her head in a bow. We all began singing "Ahkumbo." Over the microphone her voice rang out clear and true. It was a gorgeous voice and we quietly ceased singing and listened as she raised her head and with tears in her eyes—and ours—finished the song.

Kurt had felt uncomfortable about receiving bouquets of flowers after concerts along with the choir members and he thought of giving her our flowers. As members of the choir saw what he was doing, they all wanted her to have their flowers, too. The flowers were all gathered into one large bouquet and presented to her along with a choir brochure we had passed around the bus for everyone to sign. She was radiant with joy and had the bus driver thank everyone on the bus in English as she bowed and thanked us in Japanese.

There is a postscript to this story. A little over a year later, on a Sunday morning in the Tabernacle, a letter from Japan was read to the choir. It said, "To the choir members who sang with me on the bus, gave me flowers, and a program with all your names, I want you to know how I love you. I have joined the Church and was one of the first Japanese couples to be married and sealed for time and all eternity in the new Tokyo Temple."

Before the choir left Japan, arrangements had been made with the NHK television station for the choir broadcast to be shown weekly to the Japanese people. As we stood in the hotel foyer, bags packed and buses waiting, Herbert came over to Kurt and me, embraced us, and with tears in his eyes began singing, "God Be With You 'Til We Meet Again," the closing song of all choir concerts. Kurt and I sang with Herbert and bid him a loving farewell as he was staying in Tokyo to complete final TV negotiations.

Korea

Korea was our last concert stop in the Orient. Our planes flew to Seoul where emotional Saints gave us a loving welcome. Banners flew and bows and handshakes were exchanged with Saints, excited about the visit of the choir to their land. It was instant love. The choir only had 36 hours in Korea, but they were hours never to be forgotten by the beautiful Korean people nor the choir.

After taking our bags to the Shilla Hotel, we were bused to Itaewon market to shop for just one-half hour. All kinds of consumer goods could be purchased at bargain prices. The buses came to a stop and the choir scattered. Shopping was at a premium. Many articles were purchased from the brass shops at very low cost. Food markets could be seen down side streets. Vendors were standing on sidewalks selling stuffed animals and many other varieties of goods. It was very interesting to see. I purchased a beautiful white satin bedspread embroidered with roses for $12 and a leather suitcase for $10.

President Gordon B. Hinckley said, "I would never have believed how much could be purchased and packed into a bus in one-half hour if I had not seen it with my own eyes." He didn't shop, but just stood on the sidewalk and watched the circus. He shook his head and laughed at us about our shopping spree when he spoke at our dinner before the concert. President Hinckley and Elder Yoshihiko Kikuchi traveled with the choir as representatives of the Church. Elder Kikuchi sold more that 2,000 tickets, which gave him the honor of being top ticket salesman for our concerts in Japan.

At choir rehearsal in the National Theater, Oakley Evans, our choir president, told us he had been informed of the sacrifice some of the Korean Saints were making to attend our concert. Many Saints coming from long distances had borrowed money to attend and many others had purchased tickets to hear the concert on the installment plan. Tickets were $21.00 each, $42.00 for a couple. (Just think, you can hear the choir free in the Tabernacle.) We were all concerned. President Evans suggested that choir members, if they would like—and if they had anything left after Itaewon—could contribute to the Korean Saints to help pay their debt. It was spontaneous—everyone wanted to contribute. Checks were drawn on our banks at home. In the space of fifteen minutes, $3,275 was collected from choir members and their spouses, more than enough to offset the expenses of the Korean Saints.

As the choir sang to the Korean people, we had the satisfaction of knowing our brothers and sisters in the audience were enjoying our music free from debt. Many of the members brought investigators with them; most of our audience, again, were non-members.

Upon returning home, President Hinckley addressed the choir the next Sunday morning in the Tabernacle. He said,

> The choir's tour to Japan was a success with eternal consequences for those who attended as investigators and left with hearts touched by the Holy Spirit.
>
> And to all of you who were foot soldiers in this campaign goes my sincere gratitude. The pace was fast, the demands heavy, the schedule exacting. You never failed to give your best, and your best was wonderful.
>
> I know that some of you also sacrificed much to make the trip. To all of you I express the appreciation of my brethren. But most of all I give thanks to our Father in Heaven.

God bless you my beloved brothers and sisters, for your faith and devotion and the talents which you generously share. You are part of the greatest cause in all the earth. Your anthems of praise to Him, sung with such power before the beautiful people that…all of you have now come to love, were heard and acknowledged by Him who "watching over Israel, slumbers not, nor sleeps."

May the memories of this long and productive journey remain in your hearts, and may your efforts, so magnificently given, bear sweet fruit, now and for many years to come in the hearts of those who were lifted by your dedication and talent.

With a Voice of Singing—Japan

"With a Voice of Singing Declare Ye This and Let It Be Heard—Alleluia" was the theme of the choir's second tour to Japan in August 1985. The choir performed 14 concerts in seven concert halls and sang at the World's Science Fair.

New dimensions in missionary work moved forward. For the first time choir members purchased and prepared 1,039 Books of Mormon with our own personal pictures and testimonies. Four thousand brochures telling about the choir and the Church were printed in Japanese, plus 3,200 choir...Articles of Faith" cards. Several hundred choir missionary cassette tapes of "The Mormon Tabernacle Choir Sings 16 Favorite Songs and the Story of the Restoration by Spencer Kinard" were purchased by choir members to take with us. The tape gives a brief history with pertinent facts about the choir. It is a very popular tape visitors can purchase on Temple Square as a souvenir or can be obtained at the LDS Church Distribution Center at low cost. We also purchased many other cassette tapes of the choir to use as missionary tools.

Many referrals were obtained, pictures taken, and names and addresses received by exchanging business cards with the Japanese people, sharing our Books of Mormon, cassette tapes, "Articles of Faith" cards and brochures.

Arriving from the states, the choir had a two-hour delay in Tokyo airport before going on to Osaka to begin our tour. All available seats were taken in the airport. Eventually, my sister-in-law, Leona McGee (my partner on the tour) and I saw a spot to sit down on a low marble window seat, much relieved not to stand for two hours—but oh, what an interesting two hours.

Sitting next to us, a lady from the states, traveling with her husband on business to the Orient, noticed our choir name tags and began asking questions. (This was the first time the choir wore official missionary name tags with "Mormon Tabernacle Choir" printed them.) During our conversation, she revealed that Mormon missionaries had taught her four missionary discussions in her home, but she had misunderstood one phase and asked the missionaries not to come again. Talking to her further, she confided it was the Lamanites dark skin which had been her stumbling block. She felt Mormons were racial prejudiced. This opened the door so we could teach her the truth about the Lamanites that if they became righteous and accepted the Gospel, they would have a fair and delightsome skin.

The lady listened, asked more questions, and accepted our explanation of the Lamanites and other principles of the gospel. We gave her a missionary choir tape, a personalized "Articles of Faith card and she gave us her name and address. (Three months later, after she had arrived back to her home in South Carolina, I received a beautiful letter from her.)

As we were talking to our new friend from South Carolina a Chinese gentleman sat down on the other side of us. He had a two-hour layover before continuing on to Manchuria where he planned to visit his family that he had not seen for several years. He also noticed our name tags and asked about the choir, Salt Lake City and what the Mormons believe.

Just three months before, his son had been to Salt Lake City to compete in the Gina Bachauer piano competition. My being a piano teacher gave us a great deal in common to talk about. He told about his son's talent and favorable impression of Salt Lake City.

At the office where he worked in Washington, D.C. he admired and respected a fellow employee, who was a Mormon, because of his clean language and wholesome living. He also told about his Chinese friend who had joined the Mormon Church and married in the temple. Throughout the next two hours he asked many questions about the temple, Mormon beliefs, and the choir. No one had ever offered him a Book of Mormon. When asked if he would like to read the Book of Mormon, his response was an immediate "yes." He was delighted to receive a cassette missionary tape and I promised to send a Book of Mormon to his home in Washington, D.C. He was "golden" and ready to hear the gospel message.

To our surprise, as we prepared to board our plane, we found our new Chinese friend was traveling on the same flight. We laughed and talked as we stood in line, then boarded the plane. He found his assigned seat and we proceeded down the aisle to ours.

Moving quietly up and down the aisle among the choir members, I tried to find a Book of Mormon in English to give our friend. Everyone had their own personalized leather scripture sets, but not a spare English Book of Mormon was to be found. President Wendell Smoot told me he would be sure English Books of Mormon would be included next trip.

As we deplaned, and our Chinese friend stayed aboard to continue on with his flight to Manchuria, we said goodbye and again I reassured him that I would send his Book of Mormon to his home.

From this first missionary experience in the airport, we continued to share Books of Mormon, cassette tapes and printed materials with persons throughout out tour. Many were receptive to our message, wanting to know more about the choir and the Mormon beliefs.

A choir member told of her experience with a young Japanese lady who had looked all over and finally found her after our first concert in Osaka. The young lady held in her hand an autographed concert program which had been given to her by this choir member on our last tour. The Japanese lady told the choir member that the autographed concert program had become her most treasured possession. She had been taught the gospel by the missionaries after our first concert tour. She had joined the church, and now, she introduced her non-member friend who was her guest at our concert. The choir member gave the guest a Book of Mormon, "Articles of Faith" card, and choir tape.

An endowment session held at the Tokyo Temple for all choir members who desired to attend was wonderful—but and incident which happened as we were leaving was even better.

A young Japanese lady came to the temple to pray and inquire about the Mormon Church and the choir. She was hot and tired after traveling a long distance by subway, crying and excited because she had finally found the Mormon temple. A choir brochure was in her hand. Choir members invited her into the foyer of the temple. The young Japanese lady made the sign of Buddah prayer and when she finished she gave the Catholic sign of the cross. Becoming calmer, she explained that she had attended our choir concert the night before and wanted to know more about the choir and the Mormon Church. Missionaries were assigned to teach her and the choir was humbled, realizing the impact our music was having on people in our audience.

Just before arriving in Japan, a 747 airliner had crashed between Osaka and Tokyo, killing everyone aboard. Its tail section had been severed from the main fuselage. Tokyo newspapers and TV stations featured this tragic story.

At Sacrament meeting held on Sunday for the choir in the hotel ballroom, a Japanese stake president took charge of the meeting. Several Japanese saints bore their testimony with the help of interpreters, so beautiful and touching, telling of their conversion to the Church.

Brother Wilcox, a member of the First Quorum of the seventy and one of the area presidents in the Orient, spoke. He told of a special blessing given to the stake president taking charge of our sacrament meeting, who had also been given the responsibility of our choir tour in Japan. The stake president had been scheduled to fly on the 747 airliner which had crashed. At the last minute he received a strong impression not to take the flight, but to remain at the church a little longer and finish up a project he had been working on, so he called and canceled his reservation. A little later, he finished sooner than expected, and called the airport to see if he could still make the flight, but his reservation had been given to another passenger.

As the stake president arose to announce the closing song and prayer there was not a dry eye in the audience as we realized the special blessing this righteous man had received by the hand of the lord.

Because of this crash, and other recent plane crashes, all 747's were grounded and checked in the tail section area. The week we were in Japan, cracks were found in the tail section of two or three planes. The rest were cleared to fly, so our planes were safe for our return trip home to the States.

After our concert at the World's Science Fair, the choir had a special request from Japanese Television, who had helped to sponsor our tour. A benefit television show for African Relief was being broadcast. The organization asked the choir to sing as part of the program to be seen by millions of people. We sang "The Children of the World" while dancers performed in front of us, plus two other songs. It was fun—but best of all—it was an excellent missionary tool.

Our songs were heard by millions of Japanese people as they viewed the African Relief benefit program and regular Sunday broadcast. Concerts were sung to sell-out audiences, Books of Mormon, tapes and brochures placed in the hands of receptive investigators. Our hearts were full—realizing the choir had opened doors for the missionaries to teach the Gospel to the Japanese people.

Receptions were held and honors bestowed on the choir, but none can compare to the happiness and love choir members felt for the Japanese people and their hospitality.

Arriving at the airport to fly back to the States, we moved into a waiting area. Sitting on the hard tile floor at the side were a large group of Vietnamese refugees quietly eating their lunches.

We smiled at them, but they sat solemn, just looking at us. My heart went out to them. We found they were waiting for a plane that would take them to America to start a new life. After they ate, officials moved them to the boarding gate. The group was mostly mothers with small children and older grandparents. Very few fathers were among them.

Blue flight was called, the signal for all choir members on our flight to board the plane. To our surprise, the first half of the plane was filled with the Vietnamese we had seen in the waiting area. They were still solemn and unsmiling—such a big change coming into their lives.

I felt privileged to be with them as we flew towards America and freedom. As we deplaned in California, we noticed large signs being held up by their sponsoring families with Vietnamese names on them. It was beautiful to see the anticipation on the faces of the families awaiting their guests' arrival. It was a very tender time.

Blue flight was called again. We boarded the plane, looking forward to seeing our families who would be at the airport waiting with open arms to welcome us home, our job well done.

After returning home, letters were received and read to the choir in the Tabernacle. Carolyn Stock, a member of the choir, shared a letter sent to her family from a missionary serving in Japan. She had given a Book of Mormon to Elder Moffett after a choir concert to place with an investigator.

Three days ago I was transferred from Otama City to Kawagoe City, in the Tokyo North Mission. On the 30th of September I had just scheduled my first baptism as a senior companion, a beautiful family. Needless to say I was disappointed being transferred before this baptism took place and it was really hard to leave them.

Yesterday, I went to church for the first time here which is always exciting trying to put 150 new names to 150 new faces. It was a very uplifting meeting and the Lord was comforting me as I thought of the family that would be baptized in two weeks.

After church we returned home and were in the middle of unpacking my luggage which had just arrived when we received a phone call from the church. It was one of the brothers at the church saying that a man named Katayama was on his way to church and wanted to talk to the missionaries. Nobody knew him so my companion and I went to see what was going on.

When he arrived, he was talking with one of the brothers. We talked to him and decided to teach him the first discussion. We taught him about God and Christ, and he told us that he already believed that (he was a member of another Christian Church). I then told him that we wanted to tell him a special story that we knew was true and that it was about a young boy named Joseph Smith. He said, "I know about Joseph Smith. I read the pamphlet about him and I believe that he is a prophet of God. No one would persecute a fourteen year old boy like he was persecuted unless he really did see God and Christ."

By this time I was going , "OH WOW! I've heard about these stories before, but I've never seen one."

After HE TAUGHT US the Joseph Smith Story, I mentioned the Book of Mormon. He then told my companion and I and the two brothers how he knew that the Book of Mormon was God's word! He was testifying to us! He said that he read in the Book of Mormon that to know if it was true or not, to read and pray to God, and that God through the Holy Ghost would answer your prayer. He told us of his experience reading and praying and how through the Holy Ghost he knew the book was true!

I knew there was only one thing left to do, give him the challenge to be baptized. Not only did he tell us that he would, but he told us that he had intended on being baptized and joining the Church. He will be baptized on October 26, 1986.

We asked to see his Book of Mormon and found that it was given to him on September 11, 1986 by Elder Neil Moffett in the Tokyo South Mission, and that it was a book that your family, in following the word of a living prophet, had prepared with your picture and testimony. My companion, Elder Felix, and I thank you, but most of all Brother Katayama sends his love and deepest thanks for bringing to him the truth.

Thank you so much!

—Elder Daniel K. Greer

Record and Video Recording

Intensive concentrated efforts on the part of musicians and recording crews produce the beautiful Mormon Tabernacle Choir music heard on record and video today. Because choir members work during the day at their own personal professions, taping sessions begin about 4:30 p.m. and may go until midnight. Weekends are especially utilized and the results are worth it. Five gold records have been achieved by the choir as well as many other awards for their recording efforts.

Brother Richard Condie, the choir's former conductor, told the choir about his first experience recording with Eugene Ormandy and the Philadelphia Orchestra. Holding Mr. Ormandy in very high esteem, Brother Condie became apprehensive when the choir was asked to record with the Philadelphia Orchestra. He knew the choir's capabilities, but still spent a few anxious hours. After the recording sessions were completed, Mr. Ormandy told the choir, "The Mormon Tabernacle Choir is the greatest choir in the world." This was to be the beginning of many performances together.

The Columbia Symphony Orchestra also recorded in the Salt Lake Tabernacle with the choir. Later, new strides in recording technology made it possible for the choir to record "Climb Every Mountain" without an orchestra present.

To record the choral part, Jerold Ottley, our present conductor, listened through headphones to rhythmical beeps establishing the tempo as he directed the choir without accompaniment. This recording was then sent back east to Columbia Records. The director of the Columbia Symphony Orchestra listened through headphones to the tempo beeps and the choir and then directed the orchestra as they recorded the instrumental track. Orchestra and choir were now one—a new era of recording established for the choir.

"Climb Every Mountain" is one of my favorite choir records. Hearing the precision and beauty of the music—I marvel.

After the war, unable to find an apartment in Logan where Kurt planned to go to school, we went to visit friends of Kurt's family who had lived in Kurt's LDS branch in Colorado. Kurt's father had been their branch president. These friends, Anna and George Bankhead, arranged for us to live in the upstairs, part of their mother's home next door. George and Anna's young son, James, played between the two houses where we lived. Later, as my daughter Linda was going to college in Logan, one of her friends Craig Jessop, often talked to me, asking questions about the choir and the requirements to become a member. After graduation, Craig was accepted as a member of the Mormon Tabernacle Choir. Later he joined the Air Force.

In April 1985, Captain James Bankhead and Major Craig Jessop directed the United States Air Force Band and the Singing Sergeants with the Mormon Tabernacle Choir in concert, conducted by Jerold Ottley. It was heart-warming to witness, and even better to sing under their direction. Later, a bill was introduced in Congress by Senator Orrin Hatch (Utah) to make it possible for a record to be made of the music from this concert.

Senator Jake Garn (Utah) listened to choir cassettes on the space shuttle when he flew with the astronauts. Returning home, he expressed his feelings to the choir of hearing our music and seeing the sunrise as he orbited in space over the Lord's creations.

As the choir pretaped a special broadcast in honor of the Challenger astronauts who were lost, a miraculous blessing was given to me.

During the pretaping of that broadcast, I was sitting in the choir loft, two feet away from the camera. The cameraman moved in for a closeup shot, bringing the camera lens close to my face. I knew without doubt when I would be on camera during the broadcast. (Usually cameras are far enough away so a person is not aware of when they are in the camera's focus.)

Now preliminary takes were over and the broadcast began. Tribute was paid to the lost astronauts, and music dedicated in their honor. As final taping of the broadcast progressed, singing became very difficult for me. It was time for the camera to swing into my area for a closeup. My throat became very dry, choking spasms began in my throat, deep tickling of a cough in my chest was about to erupt. Miserable, my face contorted trying to hold back coughing. Desperately and silently I prayed to the Lord for help.

In seconds, a flow of liquid came into my throat, relieving strangled muscles, and as the camera pointed in my direction, all was well—the picture normal, a singer simply performing. The Lord had answered my frantic plea to not ruin this special tape which would be sent to President Ronald Reagan, to the head of NASA, and to the families of the Challenger astronauts—a broadcast to be televised worldwide.

In August 1966, the Tabernacle Choir traveled by train to Denver, Colorado. We were to televise the *Messiah* in the Red Rock Amphitheater for the Bell Telephone Hour, to be viewed by the nation the following Easter. It was to be a shortened version ending with the "Hallelujah Chorus."

As the choir walked from the buses to the open-air concert stage, it began to rain hard. In a matter of minutes we were into a real cloudburst. Some men of the choir were under umbrellas playing chess, other members huddled and talked under their umbrellas, hoping and praying for the rain to stop. If it lasted any longer there would not be time to film the *Messiah* before the sun set.

Our guest soloist came over to talk to my friends and me. She said, "What is this I've heard about the elements being tempered so the choir can perform—no matter what? Look at it pour—We're not going to get this filmed. As for me, I'm going back to Denver." —But she was wrong! The rain stopped, just like a water faucet being turned off. The sun came out. A voice was heard over the loud speaking system, "Hurry! Everyone to your places. Wipe your chairs off and let's get rolling. Time is short—no reruns. This is it!" Immediately the stage became a beehive of activity preparing for the television cut. Cameras began to roll.

Everything went well until a helicopter, taking overhead shots, made a pass directly over the choir. Wind from it's rotary blades lifted off the wig from the head of the soloist who had said it would not stop raining. We had to stifle smiles as the cameras continued to roll, but not in her direction, of course, while she retrieved her hairdo. The show must go on, not a minute to lose, no re-cut!

As the last note of "The Hallelujah Chorus" filled the air, the sun dropped behind the mountain. Our cut was completed— without a minute to spare. The*Messiah* would be heard throughout the nation at Easter time on the Bell Telephone Hour—our prayers answered.

The choir sang again in the Red Rock Amphitheater in 1984, for a single concert performance, not heard nationwide. It was raining again. Umbrellas and sheets of plastic popped up all over the packed stadium. What a lot of brave souls. The rain did not stop, but it was a fun happy time. Don Ripplinger, our assistant conductor, held a borrowed large beach umbrella over Jerold Ottley's head and music stand as he conducted the concert out in the rain. The choir was more fortunate. We were under a leaky canopy

As part of the concert repertoire, the choir sang from *Elijah*. "The waters gather, they rush along." Jerry started to laugh as he conducted us, then stifled it. We were singing and had to choke our laughter down too, keeping proper deportment. Another song about water was equally funny and by the time we sang "Waters Ripple And Flow," we all but came unglued. Have you ever tried to perform, laughing hard on the inside and singing on the outside? The concert was a smashing success. Our wet, devoted audience loved it.

The next day the Red Rock Amphitheater dried. We broadcast our regular Sunday Broadcast to an audience under a clear sunny sky.

Two Christmas stories have been recorded on video tape, "A Child Is Born," and "Mr.Krueger's Christmas." Both tapes were cut in the winter. Jimmy Stewart had been asked by our production manager if he would play the part of Mr. Krueger, but he declined. Disappointed, our production manager, who was also one of the authors of the script, went to the First Presidency telling them of Mr. Stewart's refusal.

Our production manager still felt that Mr. Stewart was the right person to play the part. The First Presidency said, let's pray about it. Soon after, Jimmy Stewart called, saying he had changed his mind. He would be glad to play the part of Mr. Krueger.

Snow was needed to portray the outdoor winter scenes of Krueger's Christmas. Our choir president asked the choir on Sunday morning to please fast and pray for snow.

For one hour into the production, we used snow machines, but in an hour, it started to snow. It snowed so much that a month later people were heard to comment, "Tell the choir to turn off the bubble machine." All levity aside, it was a beautiful time of fasting and prayer, knowing the Lord heard us once again. It was also a special time for my family. They were chosen to be one of the 27 families to be in the scenes with Mr. Krueger. This is a real family memory, caught on video for us all to remember. Our younger family are in most of the winter scenes. Kurt, myself, Susan and our three younger sons, Keith, Kay and Robert (Bob) can be seen around the Christmas tree, on the sledding hill, and helping to make the snowman. Keith lifted the snowball onto the snowman, Kay was at his side and Susan handed coals and carrots to Jimmy Stewart to make the snowman's face.

The choir received many letters telling of the joy "Mr. Krueger's Christmas" brought into their homes.

Johnny Carson invited Jimmy Stewart to be a guest on "The Tonight Show." Mr Stewart stated, "In making the film for the Mormon Church, it portrays the real reason why we celebrate Christmas—the birth of Christ."

Although Mr. Stewart worked six days on the production, he only charged for one day, besides giving all the rights of the film to the Church. He also said how great it was to lead the Mormon Tabernacle Choir.

On the lighter side, I remember a long night recording session when everyone was tired. A call came from the recording booth for Brother Richard Condie. He picked up the two part phone, put the mouth piece to his ear and the earphone to his mouth. We even have a picture. A good laugh always breaks the tension on a difficult night of recording.

When we were recording with Columbia, Tom Frost supervised the recording and Jerold Ottley conducted the music. Many jokes floated through the choir about "Tom and Jerry." Later we had a new man to supervise the recording from Columbia Records and his name was David Mottley. The jokes were then about the "Mottley Ottley" twins.

It was always exciting to hear the word's "take one" at the beginning of a recording session. Though we always hoped to get it right the first try we would often go to take two or take three. But the most exciting times of all were when we heard the words, "Perfect!—Great—It's beautiful!"

Friendshipping

The Mormon Tabernacle Choir opened the door for our family to learn the joy of friendshipping a non-member into the Church.

After our first boy, Alan, left on his mission, our family decided to work together at night cleaning a building. (We cleaned buildings to support all six missionary sons.) Children who needed to study took their lessons, then helped later. This made it possible to be together, yet earn the money needed to support our missionary.

While cleaning, we became acquainted with Bruce who stayed frequently at night in his office. Being new to the area, the only people he had become acquainted with were those at work. He lived temporarily at a hotel, but planned to send for his family as soon as he found a home to buy.

Visiting with Bruce as we cleaned his office, we learned of his visits to Temple Square to hear the Mormon Tabernacle Choir and of tours he had taken to fill time when he was not working. In our conversation he learned I was a member of the Tabernacle Choir.

Being impressed with the choir, and finding the Visitor's Center interesting, Bruce had many questions to ask us about the choir and the beliefs of our church. In turn, we learned about Bruce's family living in Illinois and the reason he was working in Utah. We also told him our family's purpose in cleaning, to help pay for our boy's mission expenses.

Speaking of finances, he wondered how the Mormon church was financed without collection plates. We explained the principle of tithing and bore our testimony that if you pay tithing you will be blessed.

We told him we had received a letter from Alan telling us his mission expenses would require sixty more dollars than we had originally planned. Worried, we prayed about our problem, and lay awake most of the night wondering what we were going to do. The next morning, I felt impressed to talk with Kurt. He was repairing a car out on our driveway, so I went outside to speak to him. While outside, one of our friends drove by, saw us and stopped. Chatting for a minute, our friends told about the building they cleaned, but had a problem on Saturdays. They asked, "Inasmuch as you have a boy on a mission, would you be interested in cleaning Saturdays for $60.00 a month?" Needless to say, we knew who had sent our friends and gratefully accepted the job.

Later, we found a building of our own to clean. This is how it has been through our six boys' missions. When extra money was needed, a way has opened and we have been able to send money to our missionaries.

We told Bruce that the Lord has helped when we sincerely needed it. Bruce listened, believed and accepted our explanation of tithing. Knowing Bruce was lonesome living in a hotel, his family being back east, we asked if he would like to come to our home for Sunday dinner. He gladly accepted. We arranged for Bruce to attend the Sunday morning broadcast of the choir and to meet me behind the Tabernacle after, to go home with my carpool.

Kurt and the children had been attending church in the early block. (Usually on Sunday, I will either attend a sacrament meeting held later in our building or the bishop has given permission for Kurt and the boys to administer the sacrament and hold a spiritual meeting in our home.) By the time we arrived home, Kurt and the children were home from church. Bruce visited with them as I prepared dinner.

When it came time to call everyone to the dinner table, Kurt and I looked at each other—we always have family prayer before our Sunday meal. We knew Bruce was not active in any religion, so we hesitated for a moment, but knew we should go ahead as usual. We invited Bruce to kneel down with our family in prayer. As the afternoon progressed, Bruce called his family on the telephone telling them about his visit to our home and how welcome we had made him feel.

Family Home Evening was scheduled that night as our week nights are filled. Again, Kurt and I wondered what to do. We found a minute for a private conference and decided to go ahead with our Family Home Evening, but with a slight change in format. Kurt found his old flannel board and pictures he used on his stake mission. We gathered our children together, explained to Bruce about Family Home Evening and asked if he would like to stay or would he prefer to go back to the hotel. He told us he would like to stay.

We began our Family Home Evening with a prayer, sang a hymn, and then Kurt gave the first missionary discussion to Bruce and our children. Bruce was quiet at first, listened, observed the reactions of the children to their father's lesson, then asked many questions pertaining to the gospel and about the Church. Later, as we took Bruce back to his hotel, he expressed thanks to our family for inviting him to our home, telling us how he had enjoyed the day. This was the beginning of many times Bruce visited our home.

The time finally arrived for Bruce to bring his family to Utah. We found out the day his furniture would arrive by U-Haul truck and informed the bishop of the ward where his home was located. Neighbors watched for the U-Haul to arrive, and called the seventy's president, who had arranged for men to help Bruce unload. They knocked on his door, told Bruce they were his new neighbors and would like to help him unload his household goods. Bruce was so surprised. He had been worried about how he was going to unload his truck. (We thought it better for people in his ward to help Bruce move rather than our family, so they would meet their new neighbors. It would also help the ward members be aware of his family. They could then be friendshipped.)

After unloading, Bruce tried to pay the men for helping, but they said, "It was our pleasure to help. Welcome to Bountiful and our ward." This was a new experience for Bruce. He could hardly believe strangers would come to help him move without compensation.

Anxious to meet Bruce's family, we telephoned to find out if they had arrived and if all was well. He invited our family to come right over, even though things were out of place.

Arriving at his home, his wife acknowledged the greeting, but immediately invited me into the bedroom. I thought to myself, "What have I done now?" Judith's first words were, "What have you done to Bruce? He wants our family to pray every morning and night, say a prayer on our food and hold a Family Home Evening on Monday nights. I can hardly believe it." To my surprise, I found out she was an active member of the Church. Bruce had opposed her strongly for her church activities and it had created discord in her home. In fact, paying her tithing had been a sore spot in their marriage. Judith said she could hardly believe the change in her husband. When they lived back east, LDS missionaries had stopped at their home. Bruce very soon let the missionaries know he was definitely not interested.

After trying to find work in California, but with little success, Bruce came to Utah in his quest for work, where he finally found a job. Judith felt the Lord led him here.

Since our children were the same age, the families became fast friends. We invited their family on several outings to the Uinta Mountains, the Manti Pageant, Family Home Evenings, and many other activities. We had a good time together. Bruce continued to ask questions now and then about the Church, was holding prayer and Family Home Evening with his family and even started paying his tithing, but was still resistant to the missionaries who had called at his home. He told them he was not interested.

The day finally arrived when Alan came home from his mission. We invited Bruce and his family to sacrament meeting to hear Alan's mission report. Bruce agreed to come and bring his family. Alan, knowing Bruce was in the audience, told of his mission experiences and also directed part of his talk to teaching the gospel to Bruce, bearing his testimony to the truthfulness of the Book of Mormon. Bruce took an instant liking to Alan.

Later, holding a Family Home Evening in our home with Bruce's family, we asked Bruce about his refusal to hear the missionary discussions. We found him still resistant, but we turned the tables on him. We said, "What if Kurt and Alan were to teach you the discussions, would you let them come to your home?" To our surprise, Bruce said if Kurt and Alan gave the missionary discussions, he would at least listen to them.

Kurt called the stake mission and was granted permission to teach the gospel to Bruce. Bruce was not a passive listener. Being a writer, he had a very inquisitive mind, asking many questions.

As his lessons progressed, he seemed to be opposed to the Church and it looked as if he would not embrace the gospel.

On the third lesson at Bruce's home, Alan had a previous commitment. Kurt and I went together as missionary partners. As the evening progressed, Kurt, Judith, and I felt a heavy stifling feeling come over the room. Bruce was in opposition to most things we were teaching. As the evening progressed, Bruce quoted Socrates and thought he had proved his point against religion. Then Kurt, to Bruce's surprise, came right back with a story from Socrates about a man whose head was held under water until his body cried desperately for air.

Socrates said, "When you want learning as much as you want air, you won't have to asked to be taught." Kurt looked at Bruce and said, "The same holds true for religion: when you want truth as much as that man wanted air, you will find it." Bruce replied, "I'm not a joiner." My answer was, "What do you mean you're not a joiner? You joined the Lions Club and volunteered for the police force." Then I paused and was inspired to say, "Do you believe Joseph Smith was a true prophet of God?" Bruce answered, "Yes"—were we surprised. Immediately the heavy atmosphere of the room completely changed like a fresh ray of light. Bruce then asked to be baptized, but we told him he would need to finish his missionary discussions.

Alan gave Bruce a crash course and finished the last three discussions out on our back lawn the next Sunday afternoon. His baptism was arranged for the next Saturday.

A year later, Bruce and Judith were married for time and eternity and their children sealed to them in the Salt Lake Temple. Their eldest son completed a mission to South America, a second son served in the Korean mission and their youngest son filled a mission to Texas. Their daughter accepted a mission call to Japan and Bruce and Judith are currently serving as stake missionaries. This makes them a 100 percent missionary family.

Bruce's interest in the Mormon Tabernacle Choir led him into the waters of baptism. The choir holds a very special place in their lives.

We Do Have Our Moments!

Choir broadcasts are televised in a very professional manner, but we do have our moments, individually and collectively.

Judith's non-member parents, who lived in New York, visited Temple Square. They had a deep respect for the choir and wanted to hear a live broadcast in the Tabernacle. After taking tours on the square, they made arrangements to attend a Sunday morning choir broadcast.

Near broadcast time, I had not yet spotted Bruce, Judith, or her parents in the audience. Excited about having them hear the choir sing, I kept looking, and finally gave a sigh of relief when I spotted them in the audience, just as Spencer Kinard was making his final announcements before the broadcast.

Jerold Ottley gave the signal for "music folders up" and "Music and the Spoken Word" began. Robert Cundick was playing the introduction on the organ, when I looked at my music to see the beginning notes and words. To my dismay, my music was upside down. With cameras rolling, music could not be rearranged. It became a case of "if you don't know it, fake it." Mouthing part of the words I did not know, singing those I did, I made it to the end of the second song, and hoped I had not been filmed by the cameras. When it came time for Spence's Spoken Word, the signal was given by Jerry for folders down and I finally put my music right side up. The moral of the story is, to quote a famous conductor, named Jerold Ottley, "Engage the mind before opening the mouth."

Judith's parents visited Temple Square several times during their one week stay in Salt Lake City, enjoying all that was offered for visitors—tours, exhibits, the Tabernacle Choir's rehearsal, and broadcast. Judith's parents said there is a special feeling on Temple Square. They felt it especially as they listened to the choir sing. They are still not members of the Church, but love the choir.

One Sunday morning my nose gave me a problem. I looked for a Kleenex—we were out. In haste to catch my carpool, I grabbed the roll end of a toilet tissue and poked it in my purse. Just before broadcast time, I sat in my regular choir seat in the Tabernacle, by the middle aisle with stairs at the side. Concerned about my problem nose, I hurriedly took the tissue roll from my purse to break off a piece of tissue, but it slipped out of my hand and rolled—a long streamer down the stairs. The roll at the end stuck to the last tissue. Cameras rolled, and so was I rolling, tissue that is, as we began singing, "Gently Raise the Sacred Strain."

Weeks passed before my friends let me live it down. Sister Jessie Evans Smith, President Joseph Fielding Smith's wife, sat across the aisle form me. She would laugh and shake her head every time she saw me for the next little while.

Speaking of Jessie, she put me in hot water more than once telling jokes to those in the choir who sat close to her. She would tell a joke, then sit sober as a judge as we laughed. Brother Richard Condie reprimanded the rest of us for not paying attention and to please be quiet in rehearsal, but Jessie was a true friend when I needed her. One of my best friends joined another church, an offshoot of our religion. My friend and her husband were trying to influence my life and thinking. Jessie was my anchor with the right answers to strengthen me.

I don't know whether to tell about my sock episode or not. Oh well, another goof I will never live down. One Sunday morning I went to my dresser drawer to look for a pair of nylon stockings. I found the only nylons left were not panty hose, but the old-fashioned separate leg hose I had planned to give to my mother. In desperation I thought, "Oh well, I'll do like we used to during World War II times, put the nylons on, roll down the tops part way, fold, tuck and anchor the tops to stay up." This used to work great back then, but I found out our new materials are different today.

Just after a concert tour and after parking my car in the choir parking lot, I filled my arms full of dress bag, clothes, music bag, and purse, to return my concert clothes back to the Tabernacle. I began walking and came to the opposite side of the street, from the west gate of the Tabernacle. Starting across the street to Temple Square gate, I felt a nylon start to slip, rearranged my load, grabbed for the top of the sock and gave it a yank up. It helped a little, then I felt it start to slip again, but in the meantime the other nylon started to slip down. Here I was, in the middle of the street, my arms full, choir members arriving from all directions coming to the Tabernacle, stockings slipping down to my buckled shoes which I could not slip off to get the nylons off, my friends laughing so hard they couldn't help me. With my face red, I shrugged my shoulders and proceeded, as is, to the choir door where the security guard, not realizing my predicament, insisted on seeing my choir pass. With arms loaded, brain rattled, unable to find my pass in my purse and nylons down to my ankles, I couldn't get in. My choir friends finally stopped laughing long enough to tell the guard to take pity on me and let me in. In my haste to hurry on to the dressing rooms, I passed by the rest room, had to stop, and backtrack to go see about my nylons. By this time my friends were almost rolling in the aisle. I went in, took off the offending nylons, looked at my snow white legs and realized this was the morning to wear short dresses. Just my luck. We have a whole rack full of long dresses, but this was short dress day.

Finally, getting my act together, I went upstairs to the choir loft for rehearsal. As the morning progressed, I could see choir members tittering and laughing in my direction as my dear friends told my story to the singers around them. Oh well, I told myself, "This too shall pass."

Once back East, the choir was rehearsing with the Marine Band in Washington, D.C. We wore a two-piece, long concert dress with a tie around the waist. Jerry asked the choir to stand. As I stood, my skirt came unfastened and dropped to the seat of the chair as I stood up, leaving me standing in my slip. Choir buddies around me came unglued and started to laugh. Even in rehearsal, we must maintain good deportment, but this was too much: they could not suppress the laughter.

Just one more, which I feel was my worst "goof," soon after I joined the choir. Some measures in music can be a bit tricky. I counted my measures wrong, sang on a rest in front of a microphone and had my solo heard all over the world. I tell my piano students they must count their music carefully. The silence in music is just as important as the sound in music.

Our choir conductors and organists are well qualified, do an excellent job, and all have a great sense of humor. They stick to business, waste little time, and accomplish much in the two hours the choir is together rehearsing, but our leaders, too, have had their moments.

If ever they slip, or twist their words, the choir is always ready to laugh along with them at their problems. Having a sense of humor will often ease an otherwise strenuous rehearsal. Tensions build and then, at the least expected moment, Jerry or Don, with their natural wit, will make a side comment putting the choir in stitches. Bob or John at the organ will play a little side melody or say something that brings a chuckle from everyone.

Several times in rehearsal Jerry has lost his grip on his conducting baton and sent it flying through the air, but when he had a baton slip and it flew through the air during a <u>concert,</u> well...! On the following Thursday night's rehearsal, Jerry walked up to his conducting podium and found a nicely wrapped package left by a choir member. Jerry opened the package, began to grin, and held up an arrow quiver full of batons to put on his shoulder, Robin Hood-style, so when he sent a baton flying through the air he could just reach back, pull another one out of the quiver on his shoulder and go on with a performance. Everyone laughed as Jerry enjoyed trying out his new toy and changing batons, but in a few minutes we were all quieted down, the quiver put away, and back into serious rehearsing for the next broadcast.

Choir members have given Jerry mint slippers for "foot in mouth" when he has had problems with twisted words, saying them wrong or backwards." At Christmas he found a jug of "bah-humbug juice" at his conducting stand to help when things become too hectic at Christmas time with so many singing commitments, TV cuts, half-hour movies, recordings, and concerts. Witches have come out from all sides of the choir loft, cackling at rehearsal and singing about witches brew at Halloween. Full-sized bunny rabbits at Easter, Santa Claus appearing from nowhere at Christmas and John Longhurst coming down from the top of the choir loft to the organ with sleighbells jingling. Bob Cundick was given a special fly swatter and dustpan to capture pesky flies that interfere with his organ playing.

At the choir's annual Christmas party, Bob Cundick and John Longhurst, who often play piano and organ duets at concerts and broadcasts, came onto the stage, in black concert dress, long tails, tie and white gloves, carrying a small toy piano on a velvet pillow, plus a very small stool for them both to try to sit on. They positioned the piano and stool just right, took off their long white gloves with a great amount of flourish, then both attempted to sit on—and finally accomplish sitting on the tiny stool together. Of course a little problem developed trying to sit there together or should I say slipping off and on the stool together, but finally they were ready to play the piano. A loud recording of their piano concert music began to play and so did they—on their toy piano—with expressive exaggeration, giving a piano duet performance as no one else could. It was about the funniest episode I have ever witnessed. I laughed until my sides ached and so did the rest of the choir members.

I'm going to tell you a story about the three bares (Feet, that is!). There was a small bare, Bob Cundick—a medium sized bare, John Longhurst—and a larger bare, Don Ripplinger.

Once upon a time in Japan, the three bares found out they had a problem. After arriving at the NHK Concert Hall in Tokyo, Bob Cundick realized he had left his small sized black organ shoes back at the hotel, but too late to retrieve his shoes in time to go on stage. There was a grand piano on stage. Bob and John were to accompany part of the music as a piano duet, but an organ loft was built above, on the wall at the side of the stage, where they were also to play. This required leaving the stage, going down a hallway and then climbing a set of stairs, in order to finally arrive at the organ loft to play an organ duet. The same procedure needed to be followed in reverse to return to the piano on stage. It was also planned that Jerry and Don would each take turns conducting different sections of the concert.

Working out a solution to the problem, Bob borrowed John's black organ shoes, only a size or two too big for him. They were to accompany the choir playing an organ duet for the choir's first number, "All People That On Earth Do Dwell." Bob would play the foot registrations; John could go without shoes and be in his bare stocking feet. The only thing seen by the audience were the two pairs of hands playing the organ, since the view of the organists feet would be blocked by a low wall. Then while Spence was talking to the audience, Bob and John would duck out of the organ loft to exchange shoes so John could play the organ foot registrations on the next segment of songs. This worked fine except for the time element. It took so long to exchange shoes, that Bob and John did not have time to check the organ registrations. Thus, "Faith of Our Father's" began with brilliant horizontal trumpets blasting the air. Recovering from this display, Bob and John continued to accompany the choir through the hymn group without incident. The next maneuver required another shoe change between Bob and John. After it was accomplished, Bob hurried down to the stage, where he accompanied the choir on the piano in his original composition, "Song of the Heart" (incidentally, if you have not had the privilege of hearing it yet, you have missed hearing a beautiful song).

It was now intermission. By this time the choir knew something strange had been going on which was confirmed as we all went backstage and very quietly laughed at the situation as it had progressed so far. But there was more to come. Bob and John were so relieved they had made it through the first half of the program, and then were so distracted by the laughing members of the choir, that they forgot to thoroughly think through the second half of the concert.

Bob had the shoes on, but John needed to go on stage with Bob to play a piano duet for the next section of numbers. Bare stocking feet—what to do? Ah! there is Don standing backstage with the only available pair of nice black shoes, only two sizes too large. They would have to do. But there was a problem with this arrangement. Don had to go on stage immediately afterwards to conduct the next section, a medley of Disney songs. The three bares went backstage, realized the last number would have to be accompanied by piano, requiring a three-way switch. John took off Don's shoes, Bob returned John's shoes and Bob put on his street shoes. The final numbers finished and bows were taken. As soon as they were backstage, not within hearing distance of the audience, the choir members broke into peals of laughter.

For the evening concert, Bob's shoes were delivered from the hotel, his bare feet finally covered. All was calm and peaceful again.

Suitcases were to be packed and put outside our hotel doors that night after the performance. The choir was traveling from Osaka to Nagoya for our next concert the following day. All clothing needed for the next day had to be out of suitcases. Guess which "bare" forgot to lay out a pair of socks to put on his feet? After the shoe episode, I won't be the one to tell, but if it will make this person feel any better, our choir manager, who made the announcement and cautioned everyone to be sure to keep everything they needed for the next morning <u>out</u> of their suitcases, forgot <u>his</u> socks too. Lucky for both men, another male choir member had two extra pairs of socks. And so closes the bare sock and shoe episode.

In the twenty years I have been a member of the choir, we have had very few near misses in terms of real musical breakdown as the choir has performed. No matter what has happened from miscounted measures, or from any other problem arising in the music, the choir has always been able to recover and keep singing. You must understand that because of broadcasts, recordings, and TV special cuts, the choir sometimes only practices a piece through once or twice on the previous Sunday, spotcheck problems in a piece of music and sings through it once or twice on Thursday to do a timing run and record the song for study purposes, and then on Sunday, spotchecks are made of the remaining problem areas, the choir sings the music for a camera run, and within minutes we are on the air broadcasting. Members of the choir are well-trained musicians who have the ability to sight read music rapidly, recognize problems, and follow directions from the conductor to pull itself out of a ticklish situation—but you will never guess the song we sang and almost "crashed and burned" on. It was a near miss.

At the Centennial celebration held at Promontory Point in Corrine, Utah, commemorating the driving of the Golden Spike where the first two railroad lines met connecting East and West, everyone was in place. John Wayne was to speak; government and railroad officials were to help drive the Golden Spike; and the Mormon Tabernacle Choir would provide the music. All went well until the choir began singing, "Come, Come Ye Saints." Singing to the end of the first verse, choir members realized it had not been made clear whether, for the second verse, we were singing the hymn book version or the Spencer Cornwall arrangement. A few singers started the hymn book arrangement while other members of the choir began the Cornwall version. Needless to say, we almost met with disaster. How the choir came to a consensus of opinion, I will never know, but after almost singing to a standstill—but not quite—we all began to change to the next line, hymn book version. That is about as close as the choir has ever come to a breakdown in performance, but musicianship pulled us through.

Recently, on a Sunday morning, the technical equipment, staff and choir members all had their share of problems.

Jerry, conducting the choir, emphasized a strong feeling in the music we were singing, coming down hard with his hand on the music stand, injuring his fingers. The pain in his hand and fingers made it very difficult for him to conduct, but he gritted his teeth and continued.

It came time for the "camera runs" on "Elijah", but technical difficulties developed with the cameras and they would not function properly. On top of that, a heavy television camera on a tripod, located near the organ pipes in the stairwell, tipped over onto a choir member with a hard bang, bruising her head and shoulders. The cameraman checked to see how badly she was hurt, but she rubbed her shoulder gingerly and said that she would be alright.

Jerry just shook his head and said, "We programmed the music wrong; we should be singing the song, 'Oh Lord, What a Morning.'" We all laughed. Jerry's quip put everything back into perspective. Problems were ironed out with the equipment and "Music and the Spoken Word" was broadcast from Temple Square as usual.

But we do have our moments!

A Kaleidoscope

Like a kaleidoscope, a hodge podge of memories flood into my mind.

Kurt's first real contact with the choir came during World War II. He served as a radar operator on the aircraft carrier, "USS Roi," located far out in the Pacific. Kurt was turning a radio dial when sound waves bounced into his range and he heard, "Gently raise the sacred strain, for the Sabbath comes again," the theme song of the Mormon Tabernacle Choir broadcasts. Not knowing whether he would ever return home, he found comfort in the music as he listened, and of course, a little homesickness too. Hearing the choir was a touch of home during a very troubled and turbulent time.

When I sang in my first broadcast with the choir, Brother Richard P. Condie looked up at me and winked, making me feel welcome and a part of the choir. My heart was full.

At the general conference of the Church, choir members receive a spiritual feast as General Authorities speak, building our faith and testimonies. We humbly realize what a privilege it is to sing in the "Lord's Choir," as we are often called. There are so many talented musicians in the church all over the world. Choir members ask the question, "Why me?" But it is so, and you again silently pray to Heavenly Father for help in such a great responsibility—to serve in his missionary work—spreading the gospel to the four corners of the earth.

General Authorities always put choir members at ease, making them feel special as we visit with them underneath the choir loft between sessions of conference. We speak with the prophet and feel of his spirit, and receive the praise and love of General Authorities for the music rendered.

My family has also had the opportunity of being given a conference ticket, and one by one, sitting in the top empty choir seats at conference time—a special reward for their hours of service at home so I can sing in the choir.

After the choir sang for the dedication of the Jordan River Temple on August 15, 1981, our two youngest sons, Bob and Kay, were walking with Kurt and me back to our car. We stopped to watch a man filling in the remaining mortar of the temple cornerstone. He asked Bob and Kay if they would like to help fill in the mortar. That was a moment they will always remember.

Growing up so close to the choir—with it becoming a part of our family life—our children have not realized the magnitude and far-reaching effect the choir has on people of the world. After Alan, our oldest son, left for his mission in Washington, D.C. and surrounding area, he wrote home that he did not realize so many people knew about the choir and its reputation worldwide. On their missions, my six sons, Alan, Ronald, Dean, Keith, Kay, and Bob, have all written home telling us how being sons of a Tabernacle Choir member has opened doors and softened the hearts of their investigators. Not long ago, Bob, my youngest son, while serving in the Oklahoma Tulsa Mission, wrote home and said,

I didn't realize how popular the "Mo Tab Choir" is. It seems like about every day someone will mention it while we're tracting. Like, just the other day we knocked on a door and gave our door approach, then the man said, "Ya, isn't that the church that has that big choir in Salt Lake City?" We said "Yes." He said, "I listen to it all the time." The conversation went a little longer and I finally told him my mother used to be in it. He said he was, "privileged to meet someone whose mother was in the choir." Mom, you're awesome!

Just before this book was completed, my brother Reed called and was unable to return home due to car trouble. My husband went after him and that night Reed was reading my manuscript. In the morning he asked for a pencil and paper. I wondered why, but did not ask. After he completed writing he said, "I feel this should be shared with those that read about the choir" and handed me what he had written:

Our family was living in a small independent branch of the church in Wheatland, Wyoming where we welcomed special broadcasts from the heart of the church. One evening, our TV picked up the Tabernacle Choir broadcasting from England. The program so particularly touched me that at one point I said in my mind, to paraphrase, "Those singers have a very important calling and are going to be blessed for their service in this beautiful choir." I was thinking of all the people in the choir in general, and just as I finished passing those thoughts through my mind, the TV cameras changed the scene: There was a close up of my sister, Lela. I understood more fully the value of her calling.

Craig, my son-in-law, saw choir broadcasts at the officer's club in Korea where he served as a member of the US Armed Forces. He would point me out to his friends and say, "That is my future mother-in-law." This comment would open the door to more discussion. Craig served on a stake mission in Korea while in the service, and baptized some of his fellow servicemen and Korean contacts. He also helped with the "Tender Apples," a well-known Korean musical performing group.

Returning to civilian life and after his college graduation, Craig and his wife Linda moved to Indiana. Being a mission leader and looking for new ways to interest investigators, Craig invited me to Indiana to give a fireside or two, where missionaries and church members would bring their investigators. By telling many of the experiences in this book, I was able to help reach those who became interested and wanted to know more. (Craig and Linda are still doing missionary work. Craig tells of it in his article in the February 1989 *Ensign* called, "And How Many Children Do You Have?"

Brother Richard L. Evans was the "spoken word" of the choir for many years; at the time of his death President Harold B. Lee visited the choir to give his sympathy. He knew we would miss our friend, but President Lee told the choir, "Richard L. Evans was appointed unto death." Then looking up into the singers, his eyes rested on Bobby Mack, Spencer Kimball's daughter who was a member of the choir and said, "We know your father has been very ill, but a miracle has been wrought in his behalf, Spencer Kimball will live." (Elder Kimball later became prophet and President of the Church.) When J. Spencer Kinard accepted his calling as the new narrator of the "spoken word," he told choir members that he could not fill the shoes of Richard L. Evans, but he would walk by his side.

A most sacred concert was sung by the choir in the assembly room of the Salt Lake Temple, September 20, 1986. The choir was all dressed in white as we sang praises to our Father in Heaven.

Our spouses were the only ones invited to be with us as we sang this special concert to our Heavenly Father.

Tears were in our eyes as we began singing the opening song, "The Lord's Prayer." After the opening prayer, President Victor L. Brown spoke. The choir then sang "How Lovely is Thy Dwelling Place," the "Hallelujah Chorus," "I Know That My Redeemer Lives," "The Lord is My Shepherd," and "He Watching Over Israel." President Gordon B. Hinckley then gave a beautiful talk after which the choir sang "I Believe in Christ," "O Divine Redeemer," and President Brown spoke again. We concluded the concert by singing, "When I Survey the Wondrous Cross," and "More Holiness Give Me." At the end of the closing prayer we sang "God Be With You." Our hearts and souls were full of love for our Heavenly Father as we sang praises to Him with tear-filled eyes.

Those visiting on the square that night listened and said it was as if they could hear heavenly choirs singing. Music floated through the windows on this beautiful summer night. A night so special—it is difficult to find words to write.

At the Brigham Young University (BYU) Spring Commencement Exercises held on April 22, 1983, in Provo, Utah, the choir was particularly honored. Each member of the choir was given a special diploma equivalent to an Honorary Doctorate degree called a "Presidential Citation." A very humbling experience, a special day.

At Utah State University, in Logan, Utah, the choir and singer John Denver were to perform on March 9, 1981 in a "Symposium for World Hunger." John Denver began rehearsing a song he had written, "I Want to Live" with the choir. His voice cracked and broke. He stopped in the middle of his song, turned around and said to the choir, "You are an awesome group. I haven't been this scared in a long time." At the performance, everything went great. John Denver sang beautifully. We enjoyed meeting him. Many performers who have sung in concert with the choir have said they are overwhelmed. If the truth were known it is also an honor to perform with them. The choir has sung two other songs written by John Denver one performed on a choir broadcast and the other on the "Today" show.

The choir and the Osmond family members have performed together on several occasions. For a July 4th extravaganza held in Provo, the next year—in 1977—an Osmond family Christmas show, and so forth. It fascinated me to watch tapping signals given by Osmond family members on the backs of their deaf brothers, making it possible for all of them to sing together in proper rhythm—the music was beautiful.

We have enjoyed many special times with the Osmonds. They are great performers and friendly to work with. In Washington, D.C. at a choir concert, the Osmonds were in our audience. During intermission they came to where we were resting. I asked Donny to please autograph the choir program for my children, and as he signed it, he said, "I'm the one that should be getting your autograph. You are the one performing today." He was right in a way. Every concert we have sung, there are always those who wait in lines for our autographs. The Osmond family visited with us until it was time to go back on stage. We always enjoy being with them.

SPEBSQSA, the barbershop singing group, held their convention in Salt Lake City on July 13, 1980, filling the Tabernacle with singers. The choir and barbershoppers sang for each other and then sang together. Music resounded through the air of the Tabernacle—in fact, music came from everywhere.

Letters of appreciation and interest in the beliefs of the Church were received from barbershop quartet members.

Our contract with Columbia Records prohibited the choir singing and recording with our own Utah Symphony. But for our Utah Bicentennial tour, during May and June of 1976, the choir and the symphony were given permission to sing and play together. It was a very special time as we sang in concert with them in the Tabernacle and on tour through the state of Utah. Our last concert with the Utah Symphony was in New York City at famed Carnegie Hall on July 1st.

At the National Bus Owners and Drivers concert held in the Tabernacle, a minister from Idaho was visiting Temple Square. His son sent him anti-Church literature and asked if he would verify the material and find out if what these brochures said were true.

Before the concert, the minister became acquainted with a lady sitting next to him. In their conversation he said he was trying to find out once and for all, if the Mormon Church was as bad as he had heard and read about.

The choir program he held in his hand gave information about the choir and a few beliefs of the Church. As the concert progressed, the lady next to him noticed him write on his program, "anti-Mormon brochures are wrong and the things we have heard about the Mormons are not true. The Mormon Church believes in Jesus Christ and his teachings—it teaches the truth." Music sung by the choir reached his soul and he was spiritually fed. Again, we choir members do not realize all the lives we are touching as we sing.

At the Olympic Gala in Los Angeles held July 25, 1984 at the Greek Theater, Jane Fonda and Robert Wagner were co-hosts of the program. During rehearsal, the choir began to sing "Battle

Hymn of the Republic" and Jane Fonda cried out, "Stop! Don't go on. Wait!" She threw her script in the air and ran out front into the auditorium and said, "Now sing it so I can really hear it." We sang "Battle Hymn" and she came back on the stage with tears streaming down her face, so moved by the music she could hardly speak. This Olympic three-hour extravagnza was heard world-wide.

Driving from Bountiful to go to choir rehearsal, I went up the hill towards the state capitol building. The weather was overcast, but as my car reached the crest of the hill there was a blizzard in progress and black ice under the snow. My car started to slide down the icy hill, and other accidents had already happened on the street before me. Faced with two blocks of sliding, I knew ahead of time I would hit the stopped car protruding sideways into the road from a parking lot. A traffic ticket issued to me read, "5 miles an hour—going too fast for existing conditions." The policeman said I should not have been moving, but stopped. How could I, sliding down the icy hill? He asked me why I was out driving at all in a blizzard. I told him my destination was the Tabernacle for Thursday night choir rehearsal.

I decided to go to traffic court. The judge waived my $35.00 fine and took the points off my driving record.

Jerry Ottley said if he wanted to have a nightmare, it would be to arrive at the Tabernacle on a Sunday morning for a broadcast, take his place at the conducting stand, and find all choir members absent. (Choir members must maintain at least an 80 percent attendance record; many maintain 90 to 100 percent.) Jerry said, "What if you all decided to stay home at the same time?"

I remember a bomb threat on a Thursday night that sent the choir home early. Once, the broadcast was closed to the public when we had another bomb threat. We even had a streaker try to dart through the Tabernacle at broadcast time, but was caught.

My children remember hiding under a table during an earthquake when they were alone in the building they were cleaning for our missionary fund. I was at choir rehearsal. As the opening prayer was being offered, choir members were shaken in their seats. The prayer completed, Jerry said, "That was a very powerful, moving prayer."

After one Sunday broadcast as we left the Tabernacle to go home, we had a real chuckle. One of our visitors had taken his girl to the broadcast. Afterwards, his friends held up a gigantic heart on the lawn by the North Visitors Center that said, "Katy, will you marry me?" She was kissed, so we assumed the answer was yes—the choir even played cupid.

I have memories of the 50th Anniversary of broadcasting, on July 15, 1979, and the special program where three former conductors of the choir took part.

And I remember singing at the first Christmas lighting ceremony on Temple Square and Christmas concerts singing to people traveling from all over the United States to see the beauty of Temple Square and hear the choir concert every Christmas.

Once, at a concert back east, as the choir was filing off stage, a man smelling of alcohol and holding a small boy's hand stopped me. With tears in his eyes, he told me how deeply he appreciated our music and how it had touched him.

I remember singing the *Elijah* at the Teton Festival under the direction of Maestro Ling Tung from China.

I was lost in Brazil, separated from the group and my friends. I just had to have another pair of shoes or two. (I was fascinated by them. The prices were low and shoes well made from the factories of Brazil.) Leaving my friends, I went in the opposite direction. Later checking my watch, I realized the buses would be leaving soon. Looking around at the maze of streets, seeing people who could not speak my language, I knew I was lost. Frightened, I began walking—but where? I knew there was only one source of help, my Heavenly Father. After praying, the impression came to me to carefully retrace my steps, looking for familiar landmarks and try to make my way back. At times I would see something familiar and then other times I was puzzled and frightened. The buses would not wait. I kept going and with the help of my Heavenly Father, arrived back to where the choir buses were—just two minutes before they were to leave.

Also in Brazil, I remember hearing Eartha Kitt singing a performance before us and then later seeing her as she listened to us from the wings of the stage, tears streaming down her face.

I recall the broken down buses, and Kurt covered with grease helping the driver to fix the problem. I recall planes being grounded, but also that we have never missed a performance. We have always been there on time in spite of the obstacles.

I think of flight crews laughing with the choir after several flights, still giving the necessary instructions to the passengers: "Be sure to observe no smoking signs," "Check where the nearest exit is to our seat," and so forth. Once a flight crew put balloons all over our plane, awaiting us when we came from a concert. Choir members have helped serve food on the plane in an emergency when time was running out.

I remember how, before going to Canada for the last time, Jerold Ottley told the choir that many of us were experiencing many unusual happenings in our homes and families making it difficult to go on tour. How true it was in our case with our son leaving for his mission at the same time we were going on tour.

I think of Jerold Ottley, Don Ripplinger and our accompanists Robert Cundick and John Longhurst and the hours they have spent in special workshops up-grading the choir's musical abilities and JoAnn Ottley's many hours as vocal coach of the choir, holding workshops. They freely dedicate their time and talents to the choir. We love them for it and will always remember. I also think of Choir President Wendell Smoot and Udell Poulsen smoothing our path so the choir could perform and of our technicians always quietly behind the scenes, doing a terrific job.

Last, but not least, I remember all the beautiful people in all the countries we have visited—their welcoming spirits, their hospitality and the hours they spent in preparation for our visits wherever we have sung. We have been treated royally.

Most of all I remember the joy of singing beautiful music in the Tabernacle each week, lasting friendships made, and missionary work accomplished through the spirit of music.

Music for Canada and America

Canadian invitations for the choir to sing at the World's Fairs, Centennial Celebrations, and other important events are often combined with tours scheduled to cities in the United States. August 1967 was no exception. Choir planes arrived in Omaha, Nebraska to be part of Nebraska's Centennial Celebration. The next morning we flew to Montreal, Canada, where we sang to a sellout audience for Expo '67. Our next stop was Narragansett, Pawtuckett, Rhode Island.

All concert audiences on our tour were enthusiastic with their reception of the choir, and its performances, but Narragansett Park holds a special testimony. How the Lord does move in a mysterious way, his wonders to perform.

Three planes were scheduled to fly the choir back to the States. As luck would have it, my plane was grounded in Canada, so we went to the airport cafe for a breakfast of ham and eggs. Later, the plane sent back to pick us up served ham and eggs that should have been our breakfast—but was now our lunch. Once we arrived at the stake center, we were served a lovely dinner of ham and deviled eggs. This was our "ham and eggs" day.

After dinner, we were transported to the Holiday Inn where we deposited our luggage, and then we were bussed to Narragansett Race Stadium. Being open air, there would not be a cover over our large audience. The Bolfour Company painted the stadium especially for the choir concert. Twenty-five thousand people were expected to hear the choir's performance.

The wind was strong with dust flying everywhere. Two people held music on Richard Condie's music stand and

Alexander Schreiner's piano to keep it from blowing away. Heavy rain had been forecast for that evening. Dust blew in our eyes, wind whipped music out of our folders, and dark overcast skies threatened rain. It looked grim for a successful concert.

Brother Boyd K. Packer was mission president. He and the Saints in the area had spent many months in preparation for this choir concert.

At the end of our windy, dusty rehearsal, President Packer stood in front of the choir to offer a prayer before our performance. Addressing the Lord, President Packer gave the most powerful prayer I have ever heard. He prayed, "Our Saints and missionaries have accomplished an almost impossible task of preparing for the choir's concert. The wind and rain must stop. Over 25,000 people are expected to hear the choir's concert tonight—the missionary work must go forth to the people." President Packer did not just say please Lord help us. He spoke in a firm, positive manner: Lord we have done our part, and now it is up to you—to still the elements.

Threatening, dark skies still loomed overhead as the choir returned to the Holiday Inn to change into concert clothes. Our buses drove on the opposite side of the freeway to return to our motel. Police regulated the flow of cars. Incoming traffic jammed the freeway—cars in all lanes, as far as we could see, traveling to our concert.

During the half-hour it took for the choir to change and return to Narragansett Park, a miracle happened. Boarding buses to go back to the concert stage, we looked into the sky—stars were out, the sky clear, the air still. It was a peaceful night. We returned to Narragansett Park and sang a memorable concert, one of rejoicing and thanksgiving, knowing the Lord heard and answered our prayer. After the concert, many doors opened to the missionaries and the gospel message moved forth among the people.

Hearts were touched by music sung by the choir on our next Canadian/United States tour. Back east at a concert hall, as choir members entered the building, dissenters were at work. Word reached choir members backstage that the first three rows in our audience were filled with protestors opposed to a concert sung by Mormons. Being assigned to sing on the front row, I could easily see the first three rows of people, their faces full of scorn.

As the concert began, the protestors sat with arms sternly folded, long faces, and belligerence in their manner. After the choir sang the "Elijah", response from the audience was very appreciative—expect for the first three rows, sitting stone cold. We then sang our hymn group, ending with Spencer Cornwall's arrangement of "Come, Come Ye Saints." A spark began to flicker among the people of the first three rows, and they began to relax in their seats, the sternness in their faces fading.

After intermission, we filed back on stage to sing the last half of our concert. Things began to change. We sang "The Impossible Dream," and a few persons on the front rows began a little feeble clapping—looking sheepishly to the side at their neighbor, hoping not to be noticed. "Climb Every Mountain" came next, and three rows began to come to life, clapping, smiles on their faces. By the time we finished singing the song "Battle Hymn of the Republic," our audience jumped to its feet, clapping, shouting "Bravo," including everyone on the first three rows. Music had worked its miracle again.

Our next concert to Canada, August 1975, was to participate in the 100th anniversary of Calgary, and would prove to be a difficult one for me. My son Ron had been serving a mission in the Edmonton, Calgary area. A year and nine months had passed since I had last seen him. Of course we talked by phone on Christmas and Mother's Day, when all missionaries are given permission to call home. Finding out Ron would be attending our concert in Calgary, I asked permission of his mission president to see and speak with my son. But due to so many personal visits by wealthy parents and friends, many missionaries in the Calgary area had been disturbed by visits from home. The mission president asked Ron to be an example and not talk to me while I was in Canada. This was difficult for both of us, but Ronald understood. He would obey his mission president.

Most mission presidents, when the choir is on tour, will let the missionary visit with a parent if one comes into their area. Everyone knew before we arrived in Calgary that Ron would be in our audience, but he and I would not see each other. Earlier, I had told one or two of my friends about not being able to talk to Ron in Calgary. Before I knew it, word had spread like wildfire through the choir. I could have kept score on divided opinions as to whether I should talk to my son or not. I felt like staying in my room. I was bombarded with opinions everywhere I went with, "Are you going to talk to your boy? " or "I would not, without the mission president's permission," or "I would not matter what, if it were my boy." With 320 choir members and 200 missionaries watching to see how it came out, it affected 520 people. I also remembered, "We believe in obeying and sustaining the law."

While President Nathan Tanner was being honored in Canada, he came to eat dinner with the choir. Being depressed, I asked him if it would be permissible for me to see my son, but President Tanner just shook his head and said it was up to his mission president. I guess I had hoped to pull rank on the mission president.

After arriving in Calgary, the choir was taken to our hotel to enjoy a free evening. Two choir members, who took the part of the two missionaries in a production of *Saturday's Warriors*, knew of my heavy heart that night and invited my friends and I to sit on some carpeted steps in the back hall of the hotel. There, they performed the whole production of *Saturday's Warriors*, taking all the parts—girls and boys. It was fun, even hilarious. Many hotel patrons stopped to watch. My friends finished the play at 12:30 in the morning. They succeeded in their object of keeping my mind off not seeing Ron the next day, by making me so tired I would sleep. It did the job, but I still awoke early in the morning with a very heavy heart. I did not know how I was going to sing on stage for two hours with television cameras going without tears rolling down my cheeks. I prayed.

An impression came into my mind to open the drawer of the dresser in my hotel room. I placed my hand on the Gideon Bible. It fell open and I knew the scripture before my eyes was meant to lift by heavy heart. I could not quote it to you now, but I do know the message it conveyed. "The Lord knows of your troubled heart. You will be strengthened in the task ahead. His spirit will be with you and you will be blessed." The spirit bore testimony to me and I was comforted. I took my letter and package I had prepared for my son to the concert hall, gave it to a missionary who knew my son and asked him to deliver it to Ron before the concert.

On stage, I naturally wondered where Ron was sitting. Up on the top row of the third balcony, I saw a young man wave in a circle, it looked like it might be Ron and I waved back. It was he. Orvella Stevens, sitting next to me on stage, had spoken earlier to the mission president and as I sat looking up at Ron she told me what he had said, that "Ron was a great missionary. He has his heart in the Lord's work," and it lifted my heart. (Ron is now a bishop.) I sang with joy, without tears, knowing it was right, that the Lord was with us both. TV cameras were rolling. I marveled at the calm and peace within my soul. I could see Jerry at the conducting podium, but just above his head, three balconies up, I could also see Ron as I sang and the heaviness of my heart finally lifted. I also knew Ron had now received my letter and care package delivered by the other missionary.

It was a time of testing our faith and we were comforted.

As the concert finished "God Be With You," I have to admit tears filled my eyes. As the crowd dispersed, my friends in the choir put their heads together and quickly made up words to a familiar melody and sang it. Part of the words were, "Hello, Elder Christensen, your mom loves you and may the Lord be with you 'til we meet again." (I do not remember the reason the choir remained on stage until after the audience left. We usually leave the stage with the audience still in place.)

I'll quote from a letter I wrote to the mission president after the tour:

> While in Edmonton, the last concert before Calgary, I needed to keep my mind active and on other things, feeling a deep disappointment in not being able to see Ron—Elder Christensen. As a result, I decided to do what good I could while in Canada to help the missionary effort.
>
> At our first evening dinner, my friends and I befriended our waitress. I told her my son was serving in Canada as a missionary for our church. I explained about the function of missionaries, and a few beliefs of the Church. I asked her if she would like missionaries to call on her. She wrote her name and address down on a piece of paper for me to give to the missionaries in Edmonton.
>
> The next morning we were waiting outside of our hotel, talking to the doorman. We teased him about his pretty lace collar, he laughed and we began a conversation—you guessed it, I had another name and address to give to the missionaries. An interesting sidelight—the doorman told me his two children were going to a friend's house to hear some filmstrips that were being

shown by two young fellows dressed in suits and rode bicycles. The children were liking what they heard, but he had not invited the young men to his home—the door is now open to his home for the two young men to teach him also. His first name is Robert, and I gave his name and address to a stake president.

Choir members swarmed the gift shops many times. Bored, waiting for my friends who were still shopping, I drifted into the "Snowbird Gift Shop," at the hotel and had a very nice visit with Mary, the cashier. Mary taught languages at the university and was seldom home. She came from Austria and had heard of the choir in Europe. As our conversation progressed, she wanted to know more about the choir and the teachings of our church. She asked if the missionaries could stop by her shop and tell her more. I turned her name and address in to a stake president. Talking to him later, he said the names and addresses I handed him of investigators were already in the hands of the missionaries. All of this, because I was trying to keep my mind off the fact I would not see Ron in Calgary.

June 1983 the choir participated in the International Festival for the 150th birthday of Toronto and the 200th celebration of the Province of Ontario. The choir was enthusiastically received. Our choir president told of a young missionary who sat next to him at the concert. Our president asked the missionary how his mission was going. The boy replied, "I'm asking to be released. I am not staying to complete my mission. I'm going home." Our president told the missionary he would appreciate talking with him further after the concert, if he didn't mind. After the concert, the missionary told our president he was going to stay and complete his mission. Music again had reached the spirit.

On the same tour, the president sat next to a missionary and his investigator. The investigator was not certain of his feelings—whether to join the Church or not. As the concert ended, he told our president, "I know the Church is true; I want to baptized."

Another incident came to the attention of the choir in a letter after we returned from tour. A lady had written, "I was given tickets to your concert, not knowing what it entailed. I did not really want to go, but was pressured into attending the concert." She tells of her desire to know more about the Church after hearing us sing. She thought about it after she went home and contacted the Church to learn more. She and her husband were taught by the missionaries and they are now faithful members of the Church. She said the joy in their home since they joined the Church is boundless.

Soon after the choir returned home, a meeting was held at the Tabernacle. President Gordon B. Hinckley presided. During his talk to the choir, President Hinckley told us a letter had arrived at his office from a prominent businessman in Canada asking if the choir would return and be part of the program when the Pope came to Canada. He desired the Pope to speak and the choir to sing. The request was graciously declined. Canadians loved the choir and its music.

The Joy of Singing Missionaries

My service in the choir was coming to a close, with just a few months left to sing. Our tour to perform in Seattle, Washington and at the World's Fair Exposition in Vancouver, British Columbia in the fall of 1986 would be my last tour with the choir—but it was special.

Quoting from my journal, "Again we are leaving a son about to enter the mission home. Kay is to serve in the Roanoke, Virginia Mission. In the morning, Kay's brothers and sisters will take him to Provo to enter the mission home. Today Kay and the other children took Kurt and I to the airport to catch our flight. The choir left Salt Lake City at 6:00 a.m. on three chartered aircraft, destination, Vancouver, B.C.

Buses met the choir at the airport where we were taken to Seattle, Washington for the first concert of our tour. Arriving at our hotel, we had two-and-a-half hours of free time, so Kurt and I went out of the hotel to look for a restaurant. Meeting friends who were going to the Fisherman's Market at the bottom of the hill, we ran to catch the bus.

We found a place to eat by the wharf, then Kurt and I began walking, looking at the shops. As we walked, I realized this was the same market I had visited five years previously. Things began to click into place.

Above my desk at work hangs a poem that has lifted my spirit many times on difficult and trying days. A woman in this same market had given me the poem on our last tour five years ago. It is called, "There's Sunshine in a Smile."

There's Sunshine In a Smile

Life is a mixture
>of sunshine and rain
Laughter and pleasure,
>teardrops and pain,
All days can't be bright,
>but it's certainly true,
There was never a cloud
>the sun didn't shine through—
So just keep on smiling
>whatever betide you,
Secure in the knowledge
>God is always beside you,
And you'll find when you smile
>your day will be brighter
And all of your burdens
>will seem so much lighter—
For each time you smile
>you will find it true
Somebody, Somewhere
>will Smile Back At You,
And nothing on earth
>can make life more worthwhile
Than the sunshine and warmth
>of a Beautiful Smile

Her name was Lela—the same as mine. I have seldom met anyone with my identical name. Originally this is what had attracted me to her shop.

Visiting with her, I read this poem where it was lying under a glass on her store counter. Impressed with it, I asked for a copy. She told me that whenever she was blue or discouraged she thought of the words in the poem and her burden would seem a little lighter, life easier to bear. Her husband was confined to a wheelchair and she provided a living for them from her little shop.

At that time, our meeting was brief, only fifteen minutes, but she touched my life. Through the years I have thought of Lela and wondered about her. When you have traveled many places and seen many shops, memory can be a little blurred. I told Kurt I felt Lela's shop was on the lower floor and asked if we could go thank her for her poem. Missing the shop at first, I remembered it was located on a corner. We looked, but the corner shop had white covers over its goods and the proprietor gone—no shop name. I told Kurt this looked like the right place, but I wasn't sure—then I spotted a faded poem under the glass. This was it—I knew for sure, but where was Lela?

We inquired around the other shops, but no one knew of Lela's whereabouts. Her shop had been closed for days. The "hippy" shop keeper next door said, "She's an evil woman; she thought I stole her friend's shop and I won't tell you a thing about her." This shook me, but I continued to inquire at another shop or two, to no avail.

About to give up, because our time was running short, I tried one more shop across the way. When I asked for Lela, he said, "Oh, I pick up her mail all of the time for her. Lela's husband died two months ago and she had a heart attack last month. She is at home in her apartment, ill." He reassured me that Lela was a very nice person, alone now, family gone, and very few friends. She had no phone, and he couldn't give me an exact address. My time was up, but I asked for a pencil and paper to write her a note. I wanted Lela to know how her courage and poem had affected my life. I also left a choir cassette missionary tape filled with music, and the spoken word by Spencer Kinard, telling the story of the Restoration and a choir "Article of Faith" card.

The helpful shopkeeper said he would see that Lela received my note, tape, and card. He knew it would be a comfort to her to know someone cared.

It was almost as if I had been led to her shop to leave my word of greeting. Finding Lela's shop and finally being able to thank her for her uplifting poem really meant a lot to me.

We then went back to our hotel, changed clothes and boarded buses for the concert hall where we sang to a scll-out audience in Seattle. The next morning we left by boat for Victoria Island and visited beautiful Butchart Gardens. It was a fun, delightful day—a time to rest.

Arriving back in Vancouver at our hotels, we unpacked. For the next three nights we were to sing concerts at the World's Fair, but in the daytime we had free time to see the fair. Talking to people as we all stood in line to see the exhibits, people noticed our choir identification tags. They asked questions about the choir and the Church. Many said they listened to the choir every Sunday. They were not members, but enjoyed our music. We gave them choir missionary tapes and "Articles of Faith" cards.

My daughter and son-in-law, Linda and Craig, called several times at home before we left, co-ordinating our visit to Vancouver where Craig's father, his step-mother, and 93-year-old grandmother lived. Being non-members, the choir is about the only thing they knew about the Church. Kurt and I had never met Craig's dad or grandmother even though Craig and Linda had been married for ten years. His dad did not come to the wedding held in the Salt Lake Temple.

After asking Udell Poulsen, our choir manager, about obtaining tickets for Craig's family to attend the Sunday morning broadcast and short concert to be sung afterwards in the Orpheum Theater, Udell had me call Brother Ray L. Dykes, who was the Church Public Communications Director for British Columbia.

Because Craig's folks were non-members, we were able to obtain tickets for the broadcast and mini-concert afterwards. Brother Dykes sent the tickets directly to Craig's folks.

According to the contracts with the Expo, the broadcast could not be treated in any was as a concert, so it was first-come, first-serve seating. No tickets were issued for the balcony—it was to be left empty. Ushers could not be used. One thousand tickets were allowed to be given out, even though the theater had a much larger capacity. Expo did not allow this "free concert," as they called it, to be in competition with the concerts at the fair. All evening performances were sold out and just a very few tickets not sold for the Saturday matinee. As long as all concerts were not sold out, the audience at the Orpheum theater where the broadcast was being held, could only use the main floor.

The day before, on Saturday, Craig's dad called and asked Kurt to go to the airshow with him. (He learned Kurt worked at Hill Air Force Base and thought he would enjoy it.) The airshow was our first contact with Craig's dad, and a blessing. Kurt would not have recognized Craig's folks the next morning in the foyer of the theater if he had not seen Craig's dad the day before. Kurt led him, his wife, and grandmother to seats eight rows from the front.

The audience was full of missionaries and members with their investigators. In fact, I believe they had to have an investigator, if possible, before obtaining tickets.

On the concert stage, my place this time was center front, second row. We sang a beautiful broadcast, with musical selections especially picked to testify of Christ. At the end of the broadcast President Hinckley, who is in charge of the choir, spoke to the audience for about twenty minutes. It was a beautiful talk, geared to the non-members, telling about Church beliefs, that we are Christian, and that we believe in Christ and his ministry and the everlasting covenant of marriage. He spoke in such a way, that it sounded like a general talk to those present, but it was full of information for the non-member.

After President Hinckley's talk, the choir sang six numbers from our Expo concerts, ending with "Battle Hymn" which always brings a standing ovation and hard clapping. Then we signed off with "God Be With You."

I made my way down to where Craig's folks were sitting with Kurt and another couple they had brought with them who used Craig's sister's tickets. They were a couple visiting from California. Kurt introduced me to all of them and we talked for a few minutes and became acquainted. Then I reached into my purse and brought out three choir missionary tapes and "Article of Faith" cards which I gave to them. Inside my bag I had Books of Mormon with my personal testimony of the truth of the Book of Mormon and my picture on the inside cover of the book. After I gave them all tapes and "Article of Faith" cards, I hesitated, not knowing whether to offer them the Book of Mormon. I decided to ask the couple from California if they would like one, but they declined, saying "We already have one." Then I braved it and asked Craig's grandmother if she would like a Book of Mormon. She declined graciously, so I began putting the book back in my bag and started to change the subject. Craig's dad spoke up and said, "Could I have a Book of Mormon?" It was nice of him to ask. I was not going to ask him as the other two had declined.

We then went out into the foyer of the theater, visiting with Craig's family, and they invited us for lunch and a short drive around the city. It was my birthday. The California couple excused themselves and went on an excursion of their own.

Choir members do not leave the group and go on their own unless official permission is given from President Wendell Smoot or Udell Paulson. I found President Smoot and he gave permission for Kurt and me to leave and be away from the planned activities of the choir. Most of the choir had already boarded buses and just a few of us were left in the foyer.

As I turned to leave President Smoot and go back to where Kurt and Craig's folks were standing, a young couple about 35 years old came hurrying up to me. The lady cried, "I found you, I found you. You're not gone after all." She was very excited, then tears started running down her face. She sold me she had been looking all over and thought she had missed me, that I was her favorite star of the choir broadcast. She said she enjoyed watching me on TV as I had such an expressive face that conveyed the feeling of the music and she always looked for me on a broadcast. She especially wanted to see and meet me and asked for my autograph—then as she was talking, another lady spoke up from a little distance away and said, "I couldn't help hearing what she said and I want you to know that I agree with her. Your face radiates when you sing. Today during the broadcast you, and the person standing next to you (Annette West), stood out from the crowd." By this time I was so choked up I could hardly talk.

As I walked away from the concert stage I knew I would never sing with the choir away from home again. This was my last concert on tour. The ladies saying these kind things, that had never been said to me before at any other concert, was as if Heavenly Father knew, and had led them to me. It was a difficult moment for me as I was leaving the theater.

I thanked both ladies, gave them both hugs, with tears in all our eyes, and let them know how much their words meant to me. To be singled out from over 325 singers is special. It was also a very emotional experience for both of them, to let me know they enjoyed watching me sing. I knew within my heart I had been able to reach the hearts of others through song, and that is what the choir and its music is all about. This was a very special, spiritual experience for me and not to be taken lightly. It gives me a feeling of deep responsibility to know there are those listening to our TV broadcasts who do pick us out individually while we sing. The first lady and her husband stayed to talk and I invited her to come over and meet our guests and Kurt. After introductions were completed, she told them about her happiness in finding me and the reason. Instead of just an autograph, I gave her a choir tape and my personal "Articles of Faith" card with my name and address on it. I told her I would write to her when I arrived home (we still keep in touch). She was so happy, she started to cry. She showed me the pictures of her three children. About this time, her husband, being concerned she was taking too much of our time (which she wasn't), encouraged her to tell us goodbye. She had a hard time leaving and we said goodbye with much love.

As Kurt and I and Craig's folks left the theater and waited to cross the street, we heard another person call, "Wait, don't go, please let me see you." We stopped and a lady ran to us and said, "I've been looking for you and I thought I had missed you. You're my favorite person I look for on the choir broadcast as I watch TV every Sunday." It really shook me emotionally to have this same experience again. She said some other beautiful words, which meant a lot to me. I gave her a tape and card, thanked her for her kind words, and bid her a loving farewell. We crossed the street and continued onto the car.

My twenty years of service in the choir would soon be over. This was my last broadcast away from home on a choir tour. To have these three persons come up and express how they felt about me, at my last broadcast, touched my heart and spirit, helping me realize that no matter where I have gone or sung, there are those who watch and care. I was very glad my performance had been such, that they had been uplifted spiritually. It made me feel humble, and prayerful that I would never let anyone down, but continue to reach the people in the few months left.

"A song of the righteous is a prayer unto me," the Lord has said. May it always be true that all members of the choir may sing and reach the hearts of the people.

This tour to Canada was a very wonderful and spiritual experience for all the choir. We were able to reach the hearts of many people and open the doors for the missionaries to preach the gospel.

In my journal at this point (long before the collapse of communism, remember) I wrote;

After the salmon dinner at the stake center in Victoria, we held a short meeting with the Saints. We met in the chapei. Brother Howard Biddulph, Regional Representative for Canada, spoke, telling of his trip to the Soviet Union. In a conversation he had with a priest, the priest said, "So you belong to the church with the heavenly choir." Brother Biddulph asked, "What choir is that?" and the Russian priest replied, "The one in Salt Lake City."

Brother Biddulph spoke to many persons in the Soviet Union who had heard of the Mormon Tabernacle Choir and its music. Even though our records cannot be sold in that country or our broadcasts heard, many in the Soviet Union hear the choir over Radio Free Europe.

At our meeting with the Saints of Victoria, our conductor, Jerold Ottley, led the choir in "When I Survey the Wondrous Cross." We stood interspersed among the audience of the chapel and the cultural hall. There was not a dry eye in the audience or the choir, as we sang to the Saints, of our Savior, in our sister land, Canada.

Before the choir left Vancouver to return home, President Hinckley spoke to us. In his talk he said, "It has been a great compliment to the choir to sing at the Exposition to a sell-out audience in competition with the "scream machine" (roller coaster) and the Lion's ball game across the way from where the choir sang. The choir left a great impression in a moving way, leaving a new message at Expo '86." President Hinckley also said, "As in the song you sing, 'He Watching Over Israel—Slumbers Not, Nor Sleeps,' the Lord will always be there to bless and strengthen His work—that it will go with strength and vitality until it covers the earth. This is His holy work. No power can ever destroy it as long as the people of the Church live the commandments and are obedient."

Music—A Missionary Tool

Christmas on Temple Square is a special time, with its twinkling lights and fairyland of color. It was especially beautiful for me as I entered the Tabernacle to sing my final concert with the choir. My heart was full, my family in the audience, the Tabernacle filled to capacity. With the colorful Christmas trees, bowers of greenery, bright red poinsettias, and the ladies in the choir dressed in long white flowing formals, the men in black suits and white ties, a feeling of Christmas filled the air.

PBS TV was taping the choir's Christmas special with Shirley Verrett as soloist, to be broadcast next year at Christmas time throughout the nation. (All holiday specials are usually taped one year in advance. Broadcasts are heard in many parts of the world on a two-week delay basis.) For the first time a video tape called "Christmas Classics" was also being cut of the same program, to be sold in stores throughout the country. Music filled the air. The Tabernacle Choir sang songs of Christmas and I was comforted. I knew as I sang that January 18th, it would be my last broadcast and the beginning of my retirement from the choir.

In all the years I have had the privilege of singing with the Mormon Tabernacle Choir, this I know, that the Lord has been with the choir, miracles performed, and the way opened so our missionaries can preach the gospel to those who listen. I have seen the Lord move in a mysterious way, his wonders to perform.

A year later, after my release from the choir, my phone rang at work. A man was inquiring for some kind of book to learn more about the Church. I suggested Ken Miller's book *What*

Mormons Believe, which I mailed to him. He called again, requesting other books to teach him more about the gospel. During our conversation, a story unfolded of his conversion to the Church just two months previously. He bore his testimony to me.

Ten years ago, James (Jim) Casey belonged to a different church. He began asking questions, but could not find the answers in his present religion. Thus began his quest to find the truth. Jim frequented used book shops looking for information about different religions. He studied books on Islam, Buddhism, Catholicism, and many Protestant religions, seeking answers to his questions, but to no avail.

One day Jim entered a bookstore and began to thumb through old books on the shelf. He picked up a musty old book with a ripped cover, that must have been stored in the attic. He began thumbing through it, reading. The more he read, the more excited he became. Answers to his questions were found in the pages of this book called the Book of Mormon. Jim purchased this old Book of Mormon, took it home and shared his new knowledge with his family. He knew he had found his answers and the book was true, but here Jim's story ends until ten years later.

Two months before Christmas, Jim was confined to bed with a serious spinal injury. In the middle of the night he prayed a sincere prayer to his Heavenly Father asking for answers to his questions and for help in his illness. At the end of his prayer Jim said, "I received an answer to some of my questions and I also saw ladies dressed in white and men with them singing."

Jim went to the hospital and as he was checking in, they asked his religious affiliation. He said, "Jesus Christ's Church." His surgery was a difficult one, a touch-and-go situation.

After his recovery, at Christmas, Jim turned the dials on his television. On the screen were ladies dressed in white and men singing—a Christmas special featuring the Mormon Tabernacle Choir with Shirley Verrett as soloist. Jim and his family listened to the broadcast and sent for the free cassette offered at the end of the special called "Heavenly Father's Plan."

Jim called, gave his name and address. He received the tape in the mail and planned to play it while his family was away. Overjoyed by the truths he had learned, he cried. When his family returned home, Jim was eager to play "Heavenly Father's Plan" to them. As it came to the song "I Stand All Amazed" it touched their hearts as the story unfolded of the resurrection of our Savior, Jesus Christ. Jim stopped the tape and with tears streaming down his face told his family that the things they were hearing were true. They continued on with the tape to its finish.

The next day, Jim called Utah and I sent him the book "What Mormons Believe." He read it, and pondered its truths. Two weeks later two young men knocked at his door, Elder Brinkman and Elder Walker. Finding out they represented the Church of Jesus Christ of Latter-day Saints, or "Mormon" church, they were immediately invited in. Jim was delighted to hear their message. He found the Elders had tried several times to contact him—they had almost given up. Elder Brinkman and his companion knelt down to pray that they would be able to reach Jim. That night Jim answered his phone. (The phone line had been broken and was now fixed.)

Giving the first discussion, the missionaries were surprised to find Jim and his family knew almost as much about the Church as they did. The missionaries taught all six discussions to the family. Upon completing the lessons, Jim Casey, his wife Carol, his mother Charlotte, and Jim's two children Hannah and Joshua were baptized in the Church.

A year passed, and from Vermont Jim called on the phone again. He told me he was flying to Utah with his family and Elder Brinkman who had taught him the discussions. He and his family were to be sealed in the Salt Lake Temple. He invited Ken Miller, myself, and our spouses to witness the sealing of his family in the temple.

Jim and Carol's children entered the sealing room all dressed in white. Brother Robert L. Simpson, of the Quorum of the Seventy, sealed Jim and his family for time and all eternity.

As the choir was in Australia on tour, Jim and his family missed hearing the choir that had so much to do with their conversion. Jim and his family expressed their joy that a member of the choir was present to witness their family sealed.

The Book of Mormon converted Jim and his family, the Tabernacle Choir found them, touching their hearts, "Heavenly Father's Plan" and *What Mormons Believe* taught them, and the missionaries presented the discussions and baptized Jim and his family.

Jim and his wife Carol are now stake missionaries in Vermont, eager to share the gospel. They take cassettes of "Heavenly Father's Plan," "Articles of Faith" cards, and the Book of Mormon with them wherever they go, to share with those who will listen and be touched by truths of our gospel message. They now have converted Carol's parents and several friends to the Church.

Postlude

Retired members of the Mormon Tabernacle Choir were invited to be part of the 60th Anniversary broadcast, July 16, 1989. "Music and the Spoken Word" is the longest continuous broadcast in the free world.

It was an exciting occasion. President Bush, former president Ronald Reagan, and other well-known personalities gave tribute to the choir and its contribution to the people of the world.

The choir sang many favorite songs, including the choir's trademark, "Battle Hymn of the Republic." Such a stirring song—full of memories for the 400 retired choir members sitting in the main section of the Tabernacle, all grateful to have been part of such a magnificent performing group.

Spencer Kinard announced the "Hallelujah Chorus." He asked the choir and retired choir members to sing together. It was like a bit of heaven on earth, singing again in the Tabernacle under the direction of Jerold Ottley for this anniversary broadcast.

Since my release, the choir has performed in Australia and has just completed an eight country tour which included Russia.

While attending a music convention at Brigham Young University, to my delight, Jerold Ottley saw me across a large display room and hurried straight across to where I was standing. I prepared to shake his hand, but instead he gave me a hug and said, "Here's one of my favorite people. It was a joy to be remembered."

Knowing the choir had recently been to Russia, I asked Jerry about the tour. He replied, "As always, it was a hard trip, but very worthwhile." With a smile he said, "The Russian people were warm and friendly. They welcomed the choir with the same open arms we experienced in other countries. Many joyous tears were shed, lasting friendships made, and above all, doors were opened so the gospel could be taught by our missionaries."

Remembering the "European handclap" (that slow, rhythmic handclap given only rarely to a top performance), I asked Jerry about the response of the Russian people at their concerts. He said the European handclap was given at all performances. The Russian people were enthusiastic with their response to the choir and its music. He said it was a very successful tour. (A full account of the choir's tour is given in the October 1991 *Ensign* and July 6, 1991 *Church News*, and a follow up to the missionary work is being written for a future *Ensign*.)

The choir was once again a great missionary tool, softening the hearts of the Russian people, opening doors to the gospel and the Lord will continue to bless the choir as it goes forward in its missionary calling. Indeed, the spirit of music is a missionary tool.

As my friend, Jean Madsen, was released from the choir, her daughter sang new words to the song "The Way We Were." They express the feelings of all choir members as we leave.

To Choir Members, With Love From Jean Madsen

"Choir Memories"

Memories of the choir fill my mind
Many happy, joyful memories of the way we were
The great music that we all have learned to love
Songs of Mozart, Grieg and Copeland inspired above

I remember tours from the Orient, Scandinavia and Mexico
President Smoot's messages and Jerry's jokes
I'll remember, and I'll miss you.
Choir parties, Christmas time here at Temple Square
Faith promoting times that we shared
Yes, the great choir will never end
My heart will still sing with you 'til we meet again,
'Til we meet again—
Memories!

My Pathway to the Choir

Choir members are often asked how they became a member of the Mormon Tabernacle Choir.

When I am asked where my interest in music began, I can't help but think of what my father-in-law, William C. Christensen, used to say if asked, "When do you begin training a child?" His answer was "Forty years before a child is born."

All four of my pioneer grandparents were musicians. Loving music, Great-grandfather Guymon made room for his violin in his small handcart. He played for his friends to sing and dance as they rested at night from the hard trek across the plains.

My parents' home in Provo was always filled with the sound of music. Hearing mother and father sing became part of our family life. Father Lafayette C. Guymon, encouraged his children to love music, and Mother Winnie Jackson Guymon supervised their musical training.

As a small child, mother sang to me at bedtime or while she worked during the day. She had a song for everything. At happy times, she would sing, "If There's Sunshine In My Soul Today." When the atmosphere in our home became disturbed, we would hear, "Angry Words Oh Let Them Never." As we grew older, my five brothers, LaGrand, Garth Rulon, Eldon, Reed and I, gathered around the piano with our parents to sing.

Now all married, it is a family tradition to sing whenever we are together for a visit with our parents.

Even though it was the Depression years, my mother knew it was time for my formal musical training to begin. She had heard that the family who owned Stardup Candy Company was selling a very nice piano for $50.00.

Construction work was at a stand-still. My father, an electrical contractor, felt the pinch on our family budget. "I don't know why you want a piano," he said, "no one will ever learn to play it." But he loved music and decided that after all, mother was right.

Our home was filled with excitement as daddy backed the truck up to our front door and unloaded the piano into the living room.

Mother had already arranged for my piano lessons. I walked about a mile to my teacher's home each week carrying eggs and milk to pay for my lessons. After my first lesson, I arrived home, practiced my first pages of music and scrambled up the stairs to the apartment we had rented to BYU students. I excitedly said, "Did ya' hear? Did ya' hear? I can play the piano. Now listen, listen again, I'll play for you," and scrambled down the stairs to play it again for them. Being good sports, they would grin and listen. At times, when the hens stopped laying or the cow didn't give milk, my lessons would stop for a while—but I kept playing the piano.

Mother sang soprano and I sang alto, as we harmonized together washing and drying dishes. These times brought us close, singing and talking together.

Lying in bed at night, I could hear my parents singing duets, daddy's beautiful tenor voice blending with mother's lovely soprano.

Playing flute for six years at Farrer Jr. High and Provo High School band (under the direction of Wesley Pearce, one of the finest music teachers in the West) was a great blessing to me. Through his teaching, I learned to count rhythm, read music fluently and interpret the written score. He stressed accuracy, intonation, and playing with feeling and expression. Several of his students went straight from our high school band into the

Utah Symphony. The years spent singing with a cappella, concert, ward, and MIA choirs (plus fifteen years as stake MIA and two years as region music director, directing large choruses and musical productions) and singing duets and trios with family and friends gave me a firm foundation for my future choir service.

While attending Brigham Young University, my previous musical experience was pulled together into useful tools for future callings in the Church. Professor Nelson evaluated what I had accomplished on the piano and skipped me up two grades higher in piano music. Also during that year a man who had a jazz band offered to teach me how to play the piano by ear. Florence Jepperson Madsen and her husband taught my conducting classes. Singing in the BYU Concert Choir—learning the *Messiah* and other Choral works—helped in my training for the Tabernacle Choir.

While courting, Kurt brought his saxophone when he came to see me. He would play his sax as I accompanied him on the piano or we would sing duets. Kurt has a fine bass voice. Through the years we have had fun together, singing for programs, sacrament meetings, and on other occasions.

The greatest joy of my life, besides my husband, is my family. Kurt and I were married six years before we were able to have children. In a blessing, I was promised children who would fill our home with laughter and song. In a later blessing, Elder Henry D. Moyle also promised we would have children. Within a year, our first daughter was born. We now have two daughters and six sons—Linda, Alan, Ronald, Dean, Susan, Keith, Kay, and Robert. They are all musical, have sung in choirs, and played piano, guitar, and band instruments. In a ward bulletin the bishop wrote, "Come hear the Christensen family—they are our answer to the Osmonds." Susan and Linda have their B.A. degrees in music. The boys are in the architecture, engineering, business, forestry, and aeronautics fields, and all are Eagle Scouts. The girls earned their YWMIA awards. Our family jazz band performed at many functions until the older children married. It is a standing joke in our family that anyone who is to become a son or daughter-in-law must first audition. Now the next cycle has begun with our grandchildren singing and beginning their own musical training.

Many people have influenced my artistic growth. In Logan where Kurt attended Utah State University, I had my first experience as a choral conductor. We were members of the newly organized Canyon Heights Branch for college students. I had been called as music director of the Sunday School. My first time conducting was a shattering experience. Standing up to lead the singing with unsteady legs, my heart beat double time and my hands shook like a leaf. When opening exercises were over, Brother Walter Welti, head of the Music Department of Utah State University, who was also visiting as stake music director, stopped to speak with me. It is a good thing I did not know he was in the audience or I would have been petrified. Introducing himself, he proceeded to give me constructive criticism and suggestions to improve my conducting technique. I was shattered—a complete failure in my own mind. Going home, I told my husband I would never, never, ever conduct the singing again. I spent many unhappy hours feeling crushed. However, as I thought about Brother Welti's words of counsel, the hurt diminished. I finally understood what he had been trying to tell me and recognized his desire to improve my conducting. After practicing what he had suggested at home and with my husband's encouragement, I decided to go back the next Sunday and try again.

A year later, Brother Welti once again visited our Sunday School. I tuned him out and went on conducting the music as usual. Two persons assigned to give two-and-a-half minute talks were sitting behind me on the stand. As we sang our practice songs I could hear their voices blending into a beautiful duet. As we continued the singing practice I asked them if they would mind singing the song "I Stand All Amazed" so the congregation could enjoy what I had been hearing. Continuing on with song practice, I decided to let the audience pick a song or two they enjoyed. One year of experience must have helped. Brother Welti came up to speak to me after the opening exercises and his first words were, "I don't know how anyone could help but want to sing under your direction. You radiate joy in your conducting and singing." That sentence has been indelible in my mind ever since. What a difference a year makes. What if I had stopped when I was so crushed in spirit?

In callings since, I have served as music director, organist, choral director of three different ward choirs, Relief Society music director, and MIA ward, stake, and regional music director over the Ogden area, which included my own stake in Layton. We presented several musical productions and held regional music festivals.

My first assignment as music director of our regional music festival was conducting a chorus of 400 youth singing to a capacity audience in the Ogden Tabernacle. The MIA General Board was to be in attendance. All day I had butterflies in my stomach. Frightened and apprehensive, I prayed for strength that we would have a good performance that night.

At prayer meeting before the performance, I felt a quiet soothing calm come over me. From that moment on, my fears vanished. All was well. Our concert was a success.

Soon after, the MIA General Board asked if I would lead our regional chorus in June Conference that year. After preparing the chorus, I stepped aside, and asked a member of the general board to please lead my chorus in conference as my baby was soon due.

At age 36, I decided to use a little of the money I had earned giving piano lessons to take my first formal vocal lessons. Erma Boam, who had studied with some of the best teachers in Europe, was well qualified and a very understanding teacher. After taking lessons from her for three months, I was asked to sing a solo in sacrament meeting. (I had sung solos before, but not since my vocal lessons had begun.) A lady in the audience came to me after sacrament meeting a said, "My word Lela—what have you been doing? Your voice sounds better and different." Learning correct voice placement and proper breath control adds beauty and quality to the vocal sound, but my lessons were not to last long. I was expecting another child.

During the years under the direction of the stake, regional, and general board music directors, I continued to learn many vocal and choral techniques. Ardean Watts taught me a great deal about conducting when I became a stake music director. Observing and listening to Lorraine Bowman, a member of the MIA General Board, taught me a great deal more about choral music, conducting and vocal technique. In fact, as my daughter and her friend were riding home from a rehearsal directed by Sister Bowman in Salt Lake, my daughter's friend said, "Miss Bowman's conducting reminds me of your mother's conducting."

Kurt and I moved to Bountiful a year later. One day I spoke to my husband about my desire to audition for the Mormon Tabernacle Choir. We discussed it, realizing we still had small children at home. Our children decided they could function properly while I was gone. Linda, who was thirteen, offered to take over my responsibilities and help her father in my absence. When she went to college, our three older boys Alan, Ronald, and Dean took over. The other children, as they grew, became a great help and support, shouldering their share of responsibilities.

Singing with the choir meant there would not be a mother in the home on Sunday mornings to help find clothes for the children, or to do the many small things a mother will do to make sure the family is ready for church. Every Saturday night all preparations were made for Sunday, each child's clothes laid out, two-and-a-half minute talks given to check on delivery, and the Sunday meal put under control.

Besides Sunday's rehearsal and broadcast, there is always a two-hour Thursday night rehearsal. Many extra Tuesday rehearsals are called to prepare for recording sessions and other commitments of the choir. Concert tours, shorter concert assignments and recording sessions meant days or hours away from my family.

Kurt would have auditioned for the choir, but his work changed to rotation shift at Hill Air Force Base. This was a disappointment to both of us, but Kurt said, "I'm needed at home with the children. You go ahead."

I called Richard Condie. He scheduled my audition for the next Saturday afternoon.

The morning of my audition, our family decided to go for a short trip to the mountains for a load of wood, not realizing I was allergic to the weeds and pollens at that time of year. As we came down from the mountain, I could feel my throat tightening up and my eyes were itching. I felt almost like I had a cold. What should I do? It was almost too late to call and cancel my audition. Even though my voice had a slight laryngitis, I decided to go ahead with it anyway. I went like a "lamb to the slaughter." Of course, Brother Condie was gracious to me. He played a single note on the piano and asked me to sing the major, minor, harmonic minor and melodic minor scales from that note. He checked my intervals, had me sing a solo, etc. I could sing my pitches on key—but my voice quality was gone. The weeds and pollens had taken their toll.

After the audition, Brother Condie walked out with me and stood on his front porch. He said "a letter would be sent telling me of his decision." I knew it was a case of "Thanks—but no thanks"! He continued to stand on the porch as I walked away down the sidewalk. I was thinking, "Oh well, I'll let my children take vocal lessons. Perhaps some day they will have the privilege of being in the choir." Then I stopped dead in my tracks, I thought, "No, by gum, I'm not going to put all my dreams into my children. I want to sing in the choir myself." I turned and walked back. I asked Richard Condie if he would consider taking me as a vocal student. I could tell that he preferred not to—but I persisted, smiled my prettiest, and prevailed upon his better judgement. I could tell, as he consented to give me vocal lessons, he did it with reluctance.

Two weeks later, my voice was back to normal. At my second lesson Brother Condie leaned back in his chair with a surprised look on his face. He scolded me for taking my audition at a time when my voice was having problems. I told him about our trip to the mountains and how it affected my voice.

After six months of vocal lessons and hard work, one night at the end of my lesson, Brother Condie invited me to choir rehearsal the next Thursday night, to become an official member of the choir. I was elated, but then I realized I had a problem. We were expecting another child, so I had to delay my heart's desire once more.

A year later, contacting Richard Condie, I asked him if I could resume my vocal lessons. It was not long until there was an opening in the low alto section and he again invited me to join the choir. Excited, not waiting to go home, I went on an errand to

ZCMI, found a phone and called Kurt, telling him my happy news.

At the end of my lesson a week or so later, Brother Condie put his arm around me and gave me a hug. He told me, "You're the kind of person I like to have in my choir—Lela, you are a musician." My heart soared. After my lesson, Kurt and I walked over to the temple to attend a temple session. I do not believe my feet touched the ground all the way over—my head in the clouds still remembering Brother Condie's kind words.

Kurt has a nice bass voice and later, with additional training, could have qualified to sing with the choir. But he felt a parent was needed at home with our eight children. He chose to be the one to stay home, taking our family to church, being with our six sons for priesthood meetings and giving parental guidance and influence at all times in our home. I love him for it. He has been my strong support. If ever I faltered, feeling it would be easier to stay home from a choir rehearsal, Kurt would always say, "Are you a member of the choir, or aren't you? You know your place and where you should be. If you are going to be a member of the choir then BE one."

Many sacred and beautiful experiences have been mine during my service as a member of the Mormon Tabernacle Choir. It has not all been easy. I have been re-auditioned eight different times. Periodically, both Richard Condie and Jerold Ottley have re-auditioned the choir members to make sure the voices in the choir have not changed. Medical problems, problems incident to age and many other factors can affect a person's singing voice. Periodically workshops are held to upgrade the quality and musicianship of choir members. Our directors, organists, vocal coach and several members of the choir have helped teach classes held an hour before rehearsal time. It is a continual learning and growing process.

For the first fifteen minutes after choir begins, we learn new vocal techniques and warm up our voice. Jerry and JoAnn Ottley introduce new vocal warm-ups almost every rehearsal. The musical knowledge we gain from our choir leadership is priceless. Jerold Ottley, Donald Ripplinger, Robert Cundick, John Longhurst, JoAnn Ottley and Clay Christiansen all work smoothly together with a real feeling of unity, and they are not without a sense of humor. They all have one and it can really ease the tension in a long hard rehearsal.

Many people have asked me, "Where do you sit in the choir?" We change seating periodically into several different formations. Each formation gives a little different sound to the choir, especially when we change into the "cluster" quartet formation. It gives a stereo sound with the four parts coming from all over the choir loft. Most generally we are in regular soprano, alto, tenor and bass formation. Singers are assigned to first soprano, second soprano and first and second in alto, tenor and bass, making a total of eight parts. If a musical score calls for a wider division it is done alphabetically. Singers with last names beginning from A to L take the top notes, those from M to Z take the bottom notes.

No matter where assigned to sit, I feel happy just to sing in the Tabernacle and be part of the choir producing such beautiful music and helping spread the gospel throughout the world. About five years ago, shortly before my father passed away, my mother and father attended the Freedom Festival at BYU where the choir was performing as part of the 4th of July celebration. At the end of the concert, mom and dad came down to where I was waiting. With tears in their eyes they threw their arms around me, expressing their joy at having a daughter sing with the choir and hearing a concert filled with the songs of America. I then gave my dad another hug and playfully said, "Well, dad, someone did learn to play the piano and put their music to use, didn't they?" Remembering, he smiled and said, "You are right, little sweetheart," and gave me another big bear hug.

I bear my testimony to you as I leave the Choir that music is a powerful missionary tool. It reaches deep within the heart. I know the gospel is true, Jesus is the Christ and head of the Church of Jesus Christ of Latter-day Saints. He is at the helm, so sail on to new and greater heights, Tabernacle Choir. Continue to spread the gospel throughout the world. May the Lord bless and keep you.

All my love,

Lela Guymon Christensen, Alto #62.